WE'RE PARENTING A TODDLER!

WE'RE PARENTING A TODDLER!

The First-Time Parents' Guide to Surviving the Toddler Years

ADRIAN KULP

Foreword by Bunmi Laditan

Illustrations by Jeremy Nguyen

ROCKRIDGE
PRESS

For general information on our other products and services or to obtain technical support, please contact our Customer Care Department within the United States at (866) 744-2665, or outside the United States at (510) 253-0500.

Rockridge Press publishes its books in a variety of electronic and print formats. Some content that appears in print may not be available in electronic books, and vice versa.

Interior & Cover Designer: Antonio Valverde
Art Producer: Samantha Urban
Editor: Jesse Aylen
Production Editor: Matt Burnett

Illustrations © 2020 Jeremy Nguyen

ISBN: Print 978-1-64152-795-8 | eBook 978-1-64152-796-5

R0

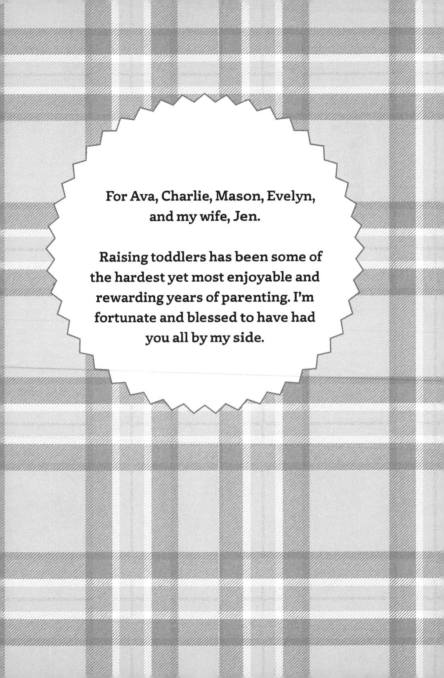

For Ava, Charlie, Mason, Evelyn, and my wife, Jen.

Raising toddlers has been some of the hardest yet most enjoyable and rewarding years of parenting. I'm fortunate and blessed to have had you all by my side.

Contents

Foreword

When Adrian asked me to write the foreword to his *We're Parenting a Toddler!*, I was immediately anxious. Because while I've successfully navigated the toddler stage with all three of my children, I've also successfully blocked out most of it.

But every once in a while, Facebook will prod my memory with a photo that I apparently uploaded of one of my children flat on their back in a pharmacy or grocery store. And while I can recognize the 2T yellow rain boots adorned with alligators, I draw a complete blank about what looks like a horrific public moment.

Nothing on Earth can prepare you for the transition from having a cooing baby wonderfully trapped in those eight-point harness bucket seats to a 30 pound, scary-strong, emotionally unstable, and surprisingly sticky human who can not only unbuckle themself as you speed down the highway, but also won't hesitate to slap you in front of your mother-in-law.

Yes, they're adorable. Nature knows what it's doing when it makes these half-human, half-hyena creatures who look like cherubs. If the chaos inside of them was in any way reflected in their appearance, we'd tap out within four business days.

Instead, we devote ourselves to teaching them manners ("Say sorry when you slap daddy," and "Poop stays in the toilet!"), raising them with love (i.e., all the Goldfish crackers they can eat), and praying that one day they'll choose to sleep in their adorable Elmo-shaped bed rather than in yours . . . on the diagonal . . . with their sweaty feet in your face.

We love them. They're hilarious. They're defiant. They're messy. They're out of control. And what they cost us in hair, undereye bags, and fine lines, they give back in slobbery kisses and adorable tushes in onesie pajamas.

Parents, you will survive this. From meal rejections (". . . but you *asked* for grilled cheese!") to pissed pants and sleepless nights, you will make it through. Even better, you'll emerge a weakened, dirtier-but-wiser version of yourself. And Adrian's wisdom and toddler war stories will be one more step to help get you through it.

Hang on. It's gonna be a wild ride.

Love,
Bunmi Laditan
Author, *Confessions of a Domestic Failure*

Introduction:
So You Have a Toddler

There were times during our first child's toddler years that I felt parenting was tough. *Surprise*, right?

I'm not sure why I expected it to be much easier than the reality. Maybe it was because I had no real knowledge of what to expect. I thought all we had to do was feed her and play with her, and life would be only slightly different. In actuality, I felt really overwhelmed.

The lists, the reminders, the sleepless nights, the co-sleeping and then transitioning our toddler to her own room—it never stopped. By the time the day was over and our daughter was settled into her crib for the night, my wife and I exhaled, made dinner, and passed out as soon as we hit the sofa.

Before I knew anything at all about parenting, my gut told me things would eventually ease up. It. Was. Wrong. Once our toddler became mobile, all bets were off. And with these tiny people, anything is possible.

Anything and everything can be put in the mouth and only retrieved after a healthy dose of fiber. The nose makes a wonderful hiding place for marbles, LEGOs, peas, and watch batteries. And what about when your son rounds the corner wearing a potty-training toilet seat stuck around his neck? Prepare yourself for a world where the outrageous becomes the norm.

A good place to start is letting go of the perfect social media fantasy world. Perfection does *not* belong in parenting.

But what we've found is our own version within the mistakes, struggles, and mishaps. We still falter daily, but we consciously remind ourselves to be present, and we're keenly aware that there may be a grand purpose behind things not going according to plan.

Coming out of my home office one day, I found a house destroyed—toys strewn across the floor, two toddlers, two young kids, a turtle, and two hungry yowling cats. Oh, and we needed to move. I shook my head, looked at my wife, and said, "It's all just falling apart." She laughed, and after several minutes, I finally joined her in the mind-set of recognizing that it wasn't all falling apart; in fact, it was all coming together.

That moment was the mental shift that we still recognize as the big turning point in our journey as parents—when we stopped looking at everything as another hill to climb and started taking advantage of the view.

That said, I'll be the first to admit that neither this book nor any other is the be-all and end-all. My parenting knowledge is a culmination of literature, watching other parents, and a constant gauntlet of guess and check. Most of the time, I fail. But that's okay. Because next time, I'll do it right.

When parenting a toddler, resist the urge to say no and invest in the power of the words, "Why not?" Give in to optimism and new experiences. Toddlers are incredible sponges, so open your eyes and try to look through those of your little one. It'll make the experience more enjoyable for all of you.

Your challenges aren't just going to be unique to your family—they're going to be unique to your individual child as well. The pace at which toddlers develop varies greatly, so don't compare, overthink, stress, or panic. Use all the tools at your disposal—this book, podcasts, other parents, your community, and your pediatrician—to help you assess if your child is on track in their development.

When you're parenting a toddler, it's important to stay consistent with major keys like communication, discipline, structure, and boundaries, but also to remember that you're human. As self-described moderates in parenting, our family doesn't always do everything the same way, and that's okay. We do our best, count our successes, and learn from the tantrum-filled moments.

If you're feeling like you're crazy, you're probably doing something right. As you may have heard, "Silence is golden . . . unless you have a toddler." Anytime it's quiet, shit is likely going down somewhere.

Parenting Books

There are countless parenting resources out there, and in my somewhat-biased opinion, you're already well ahead of the game.

Many parenting books work on the basis of discipline models from generations before you, and although there is certainly knowledge to be gained there, the world of parenting is very different than it was even 20 years ago.

This book is a compilation of the best nuggets of decades past, plus more recent practical advice. Incorporating more than just discipline, this book aims to focus on the whole child and their individual growth and development. A lot of what lies ahead in these pages comes from common sense, but that doesn't mean you won't frequently second-guess yourself. Soon you'll learn to rely on that one amazing thing all parents are already equipped with: your gut instinct.

Takeaways That Stand the Tests of Time

Interactions with your toddler over the next few years will be supremely important in creating a lasting, healthy relationship. There are some things that should generally be decided using your parental gut (not to be confused with a dad bod), but there's also a handful of takeaways that have stood the test of time. With these guidelines and your gut instinct, eventually you'll begin trusting yourself more and more.

BEWARE OF BABY TALK. As your toddler's speech skills grow, they will have their own ideas. My mother-in-law planned on being called "Laine-Laine," but her first grandson had other ideas, and "Ling-Ling" was born. As cute as it may be, my wife and I cope with how difficult it is when your child is in kindergarten and still refers to the crayons as the "caybahs."

KEEP TOY COLLECTIONS MANAGEABLE. In addition to being mindful about what you buy throughout the year, every birthday or holiday, stash a couple of the gifts they weren't *too* excited about and a few months later, voilà— they have brand-new toys.

ESTABLISH BOUNDARIES. Decide what works for you as a couple and as a family. For us, we expect our kids, aside from the baby, to start out the night sleeping in their beds, even if they eventually make their way into ours.

ESTABLISH CONSISTENT ROUTINES. Routines for morning, night, and the ever-important naptime are key. In the morning and evening, the routines we've established help all our kids, especially our toddler, understand what to expect next. But routines differ from schedules, and being flexible in the timing of your routines will help you navigate family life.

GET ENOUGH SLEEP, EVERYBODY. Getting enough sleep all around (that's right, for you, too!) can be the winning solution when it comes to behavioral hiccups and how you deal with them.

BE FEARLESS FEEDERS. Introduce an array of colorful fruits and vegetables to develop your child's palate, help their brain growth, and support their overall development.

ENCOURAGE SENSORY EXPERIENCES. Kids love anything that tickles their senses, so encourage guided sensory play whenever possible. But you'll also learn not to turn your back on your toddler. Ours loves the litter box, my wife's powder, her lipstick, full cereal containers, and anything that resembles a perfume bottle.

ENCOURAGE SHARING, SOMETIMES. Encouraging sharing has morphed into *understanding* it, and we need to be aware of how this action can be perceived by our little ones. Although it's a necessary skill, it is one that comes in time.

HANDLE TANTRUMS WITH DIGNITY. You're never going to avoid tantrums. Once you've accepted that, it all comes down to how you're going to defuse them.

KNOW WHEN TO GO. Knowing when to remove your child from a particular situation rides a fine line between common sense and experience. With time, you'll eventually be able to recognize and anticipate these situations and cut them off at the pass.

ACCEPT IT ALL WITH LOVE. I once heard a statement that's long stuck with me: "A child has nothing physical to give, so when they give you something, whether it's something they found or made or something someone gave them, they're giving you *all* they have, no matter how insignificant or trivial it may seem to you. Take those moments to heart."

The Sacred Routine

Our pediatrician shared a sacred routine with us, and I always remembered it as SEPP: sleep, eat, poop, and play. I'm sure there are variations to that sequence, but these are the components that promote a healthy and stimulated child. We have never been fans of the hard-core schedule, but a routine isn't just important for your toddler—it's good for you as well. Most of the parenting fun (and horror) occurs while you're attempting to stay on track with the routine.

This book will focus on maintaining that routine in a practical and sane way so you can provide your toddler with the basics to keep them active, alive, and happy, while connecting and bonding with them along the way.

How to Use This Book

In this book, I've created a parenting tool kit for handling common toddler behavior and navigating routines and everyday issues. We'll get inside your toddler's head so you can understand their perspective. I'll offer tips for dealing with different stages of toddlerhood, actionable methods to handle the ins, outs, and meltdowns, and stories from my experiences as a dad. With them came teachable moments and strategies that I'll share, along with when they work and when they don't, and some wisdom on how to stay calm. Read through issue by issue or start from square one and choose your own tod-venture!

PART ONE

PARENTING TOOL KIT

I've broken this book's tool kit down into four basic pillars: communication, discipline, structure/boundaries, and consistency. These pillars are strategies rooted in common sense, the tool that's guided parents for generations. By incorporating these techniques, you'll hopefully find navigating everyday challenges a bit less chaotic.

COMMUNICATION

Communication is the key to any positive relationship, and by "communication," I mean a combination of speech *and* actions. Your kids may hear you talking, but if you're not speaking to them in a way they understand, it's just your lips moving. We can't place expectations on our toddlers without properly communicating what we'd like to see. Eventually your toddler will learn that if your expectations are met, the outcome is better than if they ignore or defy you. By learning to use the four pillars, we'll eventually figure out a language that they understand—albeit with tantrums along the way, but there's probably no way you're avoiding those!

Accepting Their Feelings

Learning to accept, and then navigate, your toddler's feelings is half of the battle. The trick is in realizing when to accept their feelings and when to keep them moving. In my experience, when your toddler gets hurt—unless there's blood involved—a quick hug usually works more effectively than constant coddling. It helps them learn to self-soothe, which is a life lesson that'll take them far. We have a stockpile of cartoonish bandages and boo-boo ice cubes, and we're there to make them feel better, but we balance it with teaching them the ability to help themselves.

When It Works

When it comes to young toddlers like our daughter Evelyn (Evie), who's two, this acceptance works, but it comes with a bit of deflection because she's still grasping the concepts of possession and ownership. Lately, she's adopting favorite toys that she considers "hers," along with a tiny ice cream cone–shaped purse. If she sees someone else with her iPhone (my old deactivated one) or the ceiling fan remote, she'll throw a full-blown tantrum until that object is nestled safely back in her hands.

When that toddler fuse gets lit, I could take easy street and give "her" remote back (and I eventually do), but it would be sidestepping an opportunity. So I start defusing the situation by sitting with her alone, and though I don't totally lapse into "baby talk," I soften my tone a bit. Accepting those stormy feelings shows them that they might just be two years old, but they're still being heard.

By considering their wishes, you're showing them you respect their feelings as an individual human being. You're also building an open line of communication—a skill that'll stick with them as they grow.

When It Doesn't Work

Young toddlers don't yet understand playing together, sharing, or how to sort "good" feelings from "bad" ones. Until they're more developmentally mature, your best bet is just to encourage positive interactions.

As parents, we're learning too. We tend to teach our kids to share everything, but sometimes it's okay to have something that's just "yours." At our son Charlie's second birthday party, he received a new water float. Another little kid wanted a turn playing with it, but Charlie said no. As hard as that was to hear, he really did mean it. As parents, we were embarrassed and asked Charlie to let his friend play with it for a moment. It was almost as if the other kid knew he'd gotten one over on us, because he jetted off with it. We spent 15 minutes chasing him around the water park to get it back, only for it to have a hole. Looking back, we probably should've listened to Charlie a little better and taken full stock of the situation before making the call.

Low, Lower, Lowest: Getting Down on Their Level

Using this tool, you'll shrink yourself down to size. Put yourself in the teeny-tiny shoes of a toddler: Wouldn't it feel overwhelming to be constantly talked down to by an adult? As much as my forty-something knees complain, I'm always trying to physically get down on their level. Sitting cross-legged or holding them in my lap and connecting eye to eye pays great dividends. This easy tactic helps your child know that you are actively listening. And when toddlers feel heard, the result is always more favorable.

When It Works

I can't tell you how many times I've turned my back for just one minute only to find complete devastation. Whether Ava was upending a bottle of talcum powder onto my nightstand or smearing baby lotion all over the walls, I learned to remind myself first, not to overreact, and second, to get low. I caught my breath and sat down on the floor, maintaining eye contact and explaining why I was wiping lotion off of the walls: "Because it's for your body; our drywall doesn't need any moisturizing."

When It Doesn't Work

For me, this is the Swiss Army knife of tools—it works pretty much everywhere. If for some reason our kids aren't responsive, it's usually because of another underlying issue like fatigue or low blood sugar. At that point, reasoning sometimes goes out the window. After their mood levels out, I revisit what happened to see if I can produce a different response.

Communicating with Action

Toddlers are busy people—they don't like to be interrupted from their fun. Sometimes they need to be guided by gentle physical action, an indication that you want their attention. It can be as simple as placing a hand on their head, shoulder, or back, but it acts as a silent cue. With that light touch, they'll automatically make eye contact and slow what they're doing.

When It Works

Toddlers aren't born knowing how to clean up their play area, so showing them which things go where and asking them to mimic your actions will yield far greater results than simply asking them. It creates a moment between the two of you, working as a team, and assures them that what they're doing has your approval.

When Charlie was three, he'd be playing with his buddy Dom and get so into what he was doing that it took multiple tries for him to look up, no matter how many times I repeated his name. But making a request, combined with placing a hand on his shoulder, resulted in an immediate response.

With Evelyn, we show her how to do things through our own actions: "Evie, can you please put your shoes in that basket?" She is *sooo* excited to show us that she's capable. Showing kids how to clean up a room or do a simple chore helps them grow. When they do help, be sure to give them a ton of encouragement and praise.

When It Doesn't Work

There will be moments in which the silent physical touch won't work, like if they have friends over for a playdate or are out of reach in public. It's tough to use that brand of physical communication when they've climbed into a fast-food restaurant's playground or the elevated net-and-tube playscape at your local park. They could also find themselves in a complete state of overstimulation during a birthday party or Christmas morning—in those cases, sometimes it's best to pick your battles.

Empathize and Sympathize

We all just want to know that our feelings and opinions are being *heard*. Toddlers are no different. They need to know that we understand where they're coming from. Toddlers understand what we're saying to them long before they can speak back, so all it takes is a bit of verbal acknowledgment and blending empathy and sympathy.

When It Works

As our third child, Mason has encountered many instances where the "big kids" were allowed to do certain things that he wasn't, and this tool is clutch in managing those frustrating moments.

Recently, we were having a problem with him not understanding that his oldest sister was allowed to stay up 30 minutes later than him. We sat down with him and explained in language he understood that sometimes age comes with more privileges: "I know you're upset that you can't stay up that late. I can see that, and I'm sorry. But in a few years, you'll be able to do the same thing." It may sound crazy, but sometimes the simple route actually works.

When It Doesn't Work

Fast-forward to our Legoland family vacation, when Mason was a newly minted toddler. I swear, he was set up from birth to be a major blockhead (wait, that didn't come out right).

Mason spent the better part of his first years just trying to keep up with his slightly older siblings. At Legoland, he had a horrible time trying to match pace with Ava and Charlie—he wanted so badly to be on the rides they were on, doing the things they were doing, because he was used to being with them. Confronted with something he literally couldn't do because of his height, he entered meltdown central.

There was no way that I was convincing him with talk of feet or inches, or how it translated to the park's liability insurance. I chose to deflect and get him a cotton candy, because it wasn't his fault that he was literally too short. I didn't want it to seem like it was a reward to quell his meltdown. There's a fine line between the two.

DISCIPLINE

We can encourage good behavior, but it won't always happen. Once your child is old enough to understand the basics of right versus wrong, consider starting with some form of mild discipline along with teaching them to earn privileges instead of expecting them. With time, your child will understand that consequences come as a result of inappropriate behavior.

Rewarding Them for Being Right

A reward system can be a great source of positive reinforcement. Traditional methods *might* include the promise of a treat they don't normally get, but you can build in more creative things like playing a game or doing an activity together.

Make it even more exciting for your little one by tracking these rewards with stickers or checkmarks on a colorful sheet displayed in a visible place like the kitchen, so that they can get excited about it every time they see it.

When It Works

The reward system changed the entire scope of our chaotic mornings. Getting ready for preschool each day can feel like an epic power struggle. We were running ourselves ragged reminding the kids to brush their teeth, wear underwear, find socks and shoes, and so on.

I changed my perspective to focus on the positive and found that simple compliments really helped. Pointing out a job well done or finding the positives in their actions (rather than focusing on what *isn't* getting done) goes a long way in encouraging compliance with the daily drill.

When It Doesn't Work

You'll want to keep an eye on your child's response to rewards. When the bribe or promise of your approval is no longer enticing enough to counter the potential thrill of breaking a rule, your child may just stop listening and you'll need to change your system. The reward system can also be sabotaged by us as parents, as happened with us one morning:

Three-year old Mason and I had our morning routine, first doing the daily drop-off and then heading to the grocery store, where I got a dose of caffeine and provisions for dinner. Waiting in line to order my drink and a long-promised cake pop for the young lad, I gave him my phone and the following exchange unfolded:

MASON, AS HE LOSES THE GAME HE'S PLAYING: "Awwww dammit!"

ME: "Excuse me, my tiny three-year old son, *what did you say?*"

MASON, LOOKING UP AT ME TENTATIVELY: " . . . Dammit?"

Before I could turn a brighter shade of red, I left the coffee line.

ME: "That is a Mommy/Daddy word. That is not for little boys. I'm sorry you chose the wrong word. I can't buy you a cake pop now."

MASON, STARTING TO CRY: "I sorry, I sorry Daddy!"

After 10 minutes of crying, I felt for the little guy. He has siblings and parents that he's sponging from, so his language isn't entirely his fault. I made my way back to the counter for my coffee and, being a weakling, his cake pop.

ME: "Buddy, I'm going to get you a cake pop, because I know you understand. I know you aren't going to use that word again. Tell me what you're sorry for . . . "

MASON: "I sorry I said _____ (*completely-out-of-left-field level-up curse word that rhymes with* duck)."

Mmmhmm. I stood there for a moment, shaking my head.

The barista dropped an entire container of almond milk on the floor from laughing so hard. At this point, I was done teaching lessons. And I bought a second cake pop for me.

Setting Expectations Beforehand

Toddlers see each new experience as an adventure and have no clue what behavior is appropriate for the setting; to them, an indoor trampoline park is no different than a playdate. We all have to meet expectations in life, such as at work because there's a raise in the future. It's not much different for kids.

When It Works

Toddlers are sponges, and they'll mirror your behavior and actions. When we're cleaning up her playroom, I can say, "Evelyn, put this doll in your stroller," and she will look at me, her gears turning, before she'll take the doll and put it where it goes. Her entire face lights up when I give her praise. She knows she's done a good deed and met my expectation.

The same is true for things she knows she's *not* supposed to do, like pulling wet wipes out of the container one by one. When caught, she looks up at me with a devilish grin because she knows she's not supposed to be doing it. Once a toddler is aware they shouldn't do a behavior, it makes it easier for them to start seeing the error of their ways and understanding that a consequence will happen. Cause, meet effect.

When It Doesn't Work

Eventually you'll have a situation in which *no* expectations were met. Whether it was just a tough excursion, or you were flat-out banned from coming back again, you have to explain why and tell them you might not be able to do that again for some time because everyone's expectations weren't met.

Cut to a family movie outing and us laying out those expectations (or trying to).

"Team, we're sneaking candy in, so don't ask to buy food. You have to stay in your seats and use your inside voice, okay? Mom and Dad can't go broke buying candy for the four of you, so if you alert someone to the candy in Mom's bag, next time we won't bring any."

This ended *exactly* the way you'd expect, with our three-year old tugging at the diaper bag stuffed to the gills with snacks, using a very-not-inside voice: "Mommy, give me some candy in your purse *peeeeeas!*"

I mean, seriously, if prices weren't what they are for movie theater snacks, I'd gladly give them my business.

The Art of Distraction

Distraction is an invaluable tool to divert a toddler's attention when it comes to unwanted behavior, and many times they won't remember what they were doing in the first place. Distraction isn't meant as a replacement for discipline, but it can be used as a redirection instead of punishment.

When It Works

We joke that toddlers are the epitome of "look, squirrel!" and can be distracted by anything. Every year, I question whether or not I can finally say goodbye to the bulky, atrocious toddler gate around our Christmas tree, and every year, I continue to find my expectations not met. They become obsessed with the glittery, dangling ornaments—and what toddler wouldn't? So aside from locking the tree down, I try to distract our little ones with something with sensory intrigue of equal or higher value.

When It Doesn't Work

Occasionally, you'll find your toddler absolutely cannot be redirected. I won't forget the first time Evelyn tried chocolate. It was meant just to field her reaction, but it evolved into our sweet toddler being overtaken by dark spirits, completely obsessed with this treat. In this case, the object of distraction held more value than just a fleeting glance—it became an unhealthy obsession, and one we had to control in its own right.

A Good Old-Fashioned Time-Out

Certain moments, like when toddler fists start to fly, require removing your tod from a situation that can't be salvaged. We tend to use sitting on the stairs (in the center of the house where we can still see them but where there is nothing to play with) as time-out central. A good rule is 1 minute per age of the child, so a 3-minute time-out for a three-year-old. Time passes very slowly for these little gangsters, and after this allotted time, they've likely already forgotten why they're in trouble. This is why it's helpful to sit down and have another conversation about why they're in time-out, issue apologies, and talk about how we can avoid it the next time around.

When It Works

I use time-outs as a final resort in those inconsolably upset moments that are beyond distraction or a "go low" explanation. Time-outs generally mean that they've done something at the premium level of inappropriateness: biting, kicking, pushing down, or pulling hair. We've encountered moments when our son and daughter came to such odds that we felt like it was important to talk through the "we don't push *anyone*" position.

When It Doesn't Work

Time-outs tend to be ineffective when you've got a lot of other kids around. That centralized time-out place may now sit in the midst of the action, leaving your toddler either entertained or even teased while they're learning a lesson. And finding an appropriate time-out place is difficult when you're playing an away game at someone else's house. In these cases, it is best to remove your child from the situation, even just temporarily. If the situation doesn't improve, packing up and going home is sometimes the point to make. Parents mean business, Peanut.

STRUCTURE AND BOUNDARIES

Structured routines and boundaries serve as a baseline for toddlers, setting them up for success later on. They become conditioned to the script, making them less likely to freak out on a daily basis. And this one, I can vouch for. To this day, I never leave the house without making my bed in the morning, a habit I started when I was four years old, and it's always made me feel like I had an immediate positive accomplishment as I began the day.

Embracing the Power of No

Teaching a toddler to respect others' personal "bubbles" is tricky, but it's important, as much for the toddler as for older kids. This trait will translate as they get older and contributes to an overall respect for others. In the meantime, saying no combined with consistent follow-up will certainly save everyone from a few time-outs.

When It Works

Every day, our youngest crawls upstairs to hang out and spend time in her older sister's room, poking around in her dollhouses and toys. Ava doesn't care, but Evelyn knows that she's invading someone else's space. We generally just say no, remove her from the situation, and remind her that it isn't her room. She smiles and scrunches up her nose—she gets it.

"No" is important because your toddler unequivocally understands what you mean when you say it, even if they don't stop. As your toddler becomes older, their need to declare their independence becomes strong—even stronger than their desire to please you. And when they don't stop, you can give your no more power by physically whisking them out of that situation. No means no, Sweet Pea.

When It Doesn't Work

I'm not on that ridiculous bandwagon of asking a child if I can change their diaper. They will say no, and I'm not going to allow them to sit in a wet diaper all day. But there are times when a toddler's boundaries should be honored. When your toddler says no to a kiss, to someone touching them, or to someone invading their personal space, it's okay to remind people to listen to them. This also goes for well-meaning grandpas and grandmas, and I've had to politely ask people to give our children space because they really "don't like that."

Work Before Reward

Our kids have their own age-appropriate chores, as simple as "put your blanket in the blanket basket" in the morning or "drop your diaper into the bin." As they gain momentum through the toddler years, a checklist can help children meet expectations and achieve daily or weekly goals. We've found that with multiple children, they tend to want to keep up and even try to beat the other one, which I see as a win-win (for me too!).

When It Works

This tool is essential in the morning. We put their lists by the front door. For our toddler, it's pictures and simple sight words hung at her eye level. Evelyn learns by watching us and the older kids. Have you noticed that as your toddler ages, they start to anticipate your moves, like lifting legs to help you put their clothes on, or offering a foot to put in a shoe? This is like that, just on a newer, more visual level. Evelyn's list is comprised of simple things:

- ▸ shoes
- ▸ blanket
- ▸ bracelet

Obviously, the bracelet isn't mandatory, but she's in a season of life where she loves her bracelet. This checklist is designed not just to help Mom and Dad, but to help *her* learn what things have to happen before we leave the house.

These lists can be scaled up, and eventually the pictures are switched out with words. Once a toddler is old enough to understand routine, their to-do list morphs into helping get themselves ready, especially if they're heading to day care or preschool each morning.

When It Doesn't Work

You can start this practice as soon as your toddler begins to master word-object association, but it takes some practice. This list won't work if you try too early or they simply don't have the skills to recognize objects yet. Once our kids had that ability, it was on our shoulders to be consistent with them.

Give Toddlers a Little Control

Just like parents need to accept a child's feelings, we need to give them some freedom to make decisions. Giving marching orders to little ones works to an extent, but offering some independent choices will begin to instill the idea of mutual respect. Those independent decisions, like picking a shirt or choosing what color sippy cup they're feeling today, are big moments for them that set the groundwork for confidence later in life.

When It Works

On Friday night, after a busy week, we'll attempt to go out for a bite to eat. With four kids under 10, we don't push the limits, but even then, they're usually not thrilled. Our kids tend to see it as a playtime interruption that forces them to put on shoes.

To make it more enticing (your old man wants sushi), we often give them the freedom to choose from different sets of clothes. I've noticed that allowing them to make a simple decision sets a different tone, and they generally have a more positive attitude, which makes our meal outing more manageable.

When It Doesn't Work

Because the decisions we allowed our kids to make were never monumental, there weren't many terrible outcomes. Our biggest hurdles were not letting them wear their nice shoes out to play in the mud, or them choosing something completely ratty we thought we'd thrown away. We tried to give them full-on carte blanche, but had too many episodes of Mason wearing rain boots, skinny jeans, and a hooded sweatshirt in swampy mid-August heat.

CONSISTENCY

It's hard to do everything consistently (trust me, we've tried!) but it helps in a few key areas, like communicating effectively and standing strong on the important stuff like discipline.

Keeping a United Front

Toddlers are geniuses. They learn from a very early age that sometimes one parent says no and the other says yes. This simple miscommunication between you and your well-meaning partner provides an opening for your fast-learning toddler to get what they want, no matter if it's a candy bar, a skipped bath, or another half hour of *Paw Patrol*.

They learn who the easy target is and then they start trying to play you. In our home, Mom is the one who will always say yes to yogurt or fruit, and Dad will produce a denial. When Jen and I realized that our two-year-old was asking one of us for something and then, not liking that answer, going to the other one, we put a hard stop to it.

When It Works

After being duped by our toddler, we now have a family rule that Mom and Dad answer as one. What one says goes, and you won't get a different answer from the other. We can disagree about it as much as we want behind closed doors, but the first person to answer is the one we support. The second part of this rule is that once your toddler is old enough to understand, if they go around the first parent to another, they lose the item they're asking about, full stop.

When It Doesn't Work

The only time this technique doesn't work is when you and your partner truly disagree on something. More than once we've found ourselves trotting off to another room or texting one another in front of them as they wait with bated breath on the outcome.

You're going to find plenty of silly things that you and your partner don't agree on. What seems like a big deal to one parent may not even be on the other's radar. "Go ask your Mom," or, "Go ask your Dad," won't work—it generally pivots the child to always go to the parent who will say yes.

Consistent Discipline

Whether the consequence is constructive redirection, loss of use of an item, or a time-out, try to find some consistency. As a result, toddlers will begin to understand the consequence of doing something inappropriate.

All of these disciplinary tools generally accompany talking about what went wrong and how we can avoid it in the future. Remember the old adage, "Give them an inch and they'll take a mile." Inconsistent discipline can lead to worse behaviors and will often transcend that individual child and begin to influence other children once that trail has been blazed.

When It Works

We have a fireplace in our new house, and although the flame looks dangerous to most, it piques Evelyn's curiosity. Even the metal safety net across the front can get hot, and we never leave her unattended, but she always wants to explore and get closer. Our consistent interactions have instilled an idea that "fire" equals "ouch," and she no longer finds interest in it.

When It Doesn't Work

It's all in the balance and checking in with your partner on this one. Parenting always feels like riding that fine line between "Are we doing enough?" and "Are we doing too much?" There's a subtle difference between consistent and overbearing. The latter can begin to wear on you as the parent and can render your voice and actions unimportant.

Consistent Routine

A consistent routine creates a set of expectations in the subconscious. With routine, toddlers won't even think about doing the right thing—they'll just automatically do it. If a child knows what's coming next, they're likely to help you, or at least not fight you on it.

Our kids know there are certain sequential things they have to do to enjoy other activities, like asking to be excused from the table before going to play. The same also applies when they arrive home from school—lunchboxes go on the kitchen counter, backpacks get hung up, and shoes go in the bin. We're almost at a point where they do this without a reminder!

When It Works

By setting up a certain area for the kids that holds all of their things for school and play, we can count on them to put their things away as soon as they get home from school—even preschool.

When It Doesn't Work

Even the best routine is easily interrupted when on the road traveling or when family or friends are staying for several days. If we're on home turf, we tell our guests what we expect from our kids (like having our kids eat their dinner if they're going to have popsicles later), and attempting to keep them in a groove works out best for all of us! The reality is that sometimes the routine goes by the wayside and that's okay, too . . . because, life! Just pick yourself up tomorrow and start again.

PART TWO

ROUTINE MAINTENANCE

Routine is the gold standard in the toddler world, and most of the parenting that we do occurs within the practice of routine daily maintenance. In these foundational routines, you'll find the right structural balance to keep your toddler moving with the rhythm of the household.

EATING

Who doesn't love eating? Well, when your little tablemate is tossing your homemade pesto sauce to the dogs and offering you a slobbered-on hunk of garlic bread, you might think differently.

I'm a veteran of food combat, and I've bounced back from serving spaghetti marinara over a beige carpet. Despite the mess, eating is one of the most joyful times. Setting kids up to enjoy food and "eat the rainbow" now ensures they'll be well-rounded eaters later. Using the following tools to make eating fun, you'll make it less of a struggle for you and your littlest gourmet.

Picky Eaters: If It's Green, It's Not for Me

We all choose our parenting battles, and Jen and I decided it was important to us to make sure our kids had developed palates. Even trying to raise little foodies, we still run into issues. Ava does not eat cheese, Charlie won't eat any leafy greens, and Mason won't touch avocados. Having a picky eater is a huge universal frustration, so what do you do? Remember that small successes in this marathon help tremendously. It can be easiest to take the three or four foods your toddler latches on to and continue to serve them, and there's a time and place for that route, but it's certainly not always. We decided to tackle this issue head-on.

Evelyn developed an oral aversion after being force-fed antibiotics, so she views eating as intimidating. We're reacclimating her by showing her it's a fun process, so she's allowed to play with her food—feel it, squeeze it, and, yes, throw it. We talk to her about "kissing" her fish crackers and raisins so when she licks her lips, she understands there's something good there. It is exhausting, for sure. But raising toddlers who have healthy palates will typically guarantee they won't be the adult ordering a steak and potato dinner "with no parsley and hold the salad."

Inside Your Toddler's Mind

Your toddler doesn't understand that you're trying to help establish good eating habits—they only care about the frozen yogurt pop. "We eat with our eyes first" means that food that's inherently bright and well-plated makes us want to eat more—even toddlers. They're more apt to partake if they like what they see.

AGES 1-2

▶ Most everything hits the floor at this stage. They do well with purées, but keep them progressing. Finger foods work best because toddlers get to feel them, and kid-safe animal-shaped toothpicks are great for picking up food. But the first time your gleeful girl grabs a spoon or a kiddie fork, don't expect amazing results; Evelyn uses her dirty fork to brush her hair.

▶ They're still getting the hang of chewing, so watch them closely. Food should be bite-sized for their mouth, not yours. Keep cubes (olives, chicken, broccoli) no larger than the size of your pinky nail. When babies are first experimenting, they eat like little squirrels, "munching" with the front of their mouths, whereas toddlers learn to move food to the back and to chew.

AGES 2-3

▶ With age comes dexterity, and the use of a spoon or fork. Consider starting a healthy dialogue around food, aiming for specifics over generalities, like "This carrot will help you see in the dark," or, "This blueberry will give you a strong brain!" over "This is yummy!"

▶ The amount of food you think they need may be very different than the amount of food *they* feel like they need. Start with very small portions fit for little tummies and let them ask for more. It's best for kids to eat until they're full, not necessarily until they clear their plates.

What to Do

EAT TOGETHER. If you can, sit down as a family every night. It doesn't matter if you have one kid or nine, or if you sit in the kitchen, at a picnic table outside, or around the coffee table. Just. Sit. Together. And serve your kids what you eat, at least for dinner.

DON'T ASSUME THEY WON'T LIKE IT. On a family cruise, we learned our kids were totally willing to try unfamiliar things and complex flavors: Ava loved chicken tikka masala, Charlie would eat *any* kind of seafood, and Mason could devour spinach enchiladas. Don't cheat your tod out of exciting, necessary experiences by keeping menus limited.

FLY NEW FOOD UNDER THE RADAR. If there are "tried and true" items on the plate, slipping in something new might go unnoticed. A nutritionist friend recently told us that anxiety causes an increase in stomach acid, leading to feelings of fullness. Having something familiar on the plate leads to less anxiety surrounding mealtime.

REGULATING YOUR OWN EMOTIONS AND MOODS: WHEN HANGRY HAPPENS

I start to cook when I'm naturally hungry, but often I've allowed myself to get "hangry." Unlike my kids, I don't snack all afternoon, so I sometimes have a hard time staying stable and attentive. Snacking on the food I'm prepping allows me to stay a little more chill, so when my toddler starts to smear the wall behind her high chair with black bean soup, I can react a bit more calmly.

TEACHABLE PARENT TOOLS TO DEPLOY

These are some of the tricks we've learned that might help your picky toddler, too:

ENLIST YOUR LITTLE SOUS CHEF. Invite your toddler to help prepare a new food. Allowing Evelyn to bring her play plastic knife into the kitchen and pretend-chop carrots on her high chair tray while I prep dinner nearby keeps her contained, safe, and involved.

ENGAGE THEIR SENSES. Allow them to see and touch the food while you wash and prep it. That simple introduction can get them comfortable with a foreign food, as it's something they'll have played with even before they try eating it.

MAKE IT LOOK FUN. My wife and I have a food blog called *Think Outside the Lunchbox*, which we started when we realized the lunches I was making for the kids all looked the same: well-rounded, but *boring*. If I was bored making it, they were probably bored eating it. Presentation counts for something. Starting the blog and photographing lunches every day was a way of keeping healthyish, fun lunches going for the kids.

SUSPEND SHORT-ORDER COOK DUTY. There were certain hassle-free foods our toddlers would eat, so I insisted on making those before cooking an entirely different adults-only meal. But it wasn't fair to them to be robbed of new tastes, or to me to box myself into preparing two meals.

SERVE SMALLER PORTIONS. A tiny portion of bite-sized morsels is plenty when trying to get toddlers to sample something new. Let 'em finish it, then ask for more.

USE DIFFERENT VESSELS. Creative serving dishes can keep your kiddo intrigued! We've used everything from a vintage cafeteria tray to a hot dog dish shaped like a dachshund to a mini-muffin tin filled with toddler-ready finger foods.

GET CRAFTY WITH COOKIE CUTTERS. Shapes play to your toddler's senses. Turn cucumber slices into stars and fruit slices into trees. Let your toddler help by handing them a blunt-edged, heart-shaped cookie cutter and a slice of cheese and letting them go to town.

USE THE LIZARD TONGUE. One of our favorite means of encouraging tods to try new foods is to entice them to use their "lizard tongue" to quickly taste something, making the process more of a game. Once they saw it didn't taste offensive, we were in!

DECONSTRUCT YOUR MEAL. If you're making something like chili, save some of each ingredient and serve them, letting your kiddo try ground beef or turkey, beans, cheese, and avocado as separate bites. Next time, give it to them mixed together!

WHEN SH*T HITS THE FAN

When your child won't eat, it could be a bellyache, sore throat, or just a phase. Offering foods with varying textures gives your child some options. Keep being a good role model, continue serving a variety of foods, and don't create a power struggle. If you feel like there may be an underlying issue beyond pure stubbornness, talk to the pediatrician.

The Never-Ending Snack Cup

Oversnacking didn't really occur for us until Ava was three. She'd literally snack nonstop, with cheddar fish crackers or bunny grahams on tap all day. We got into a pattern where she'd eat these tiny meals, and then 15 minutes later ask for a snack. It felt like she was eating more out of boredom than hunger, and then Charlie got into it, too.

Behold the result of the never-ending snack: Come dinnertime, no one ate a thing. We'd allowed them to pump themselves full of so many snacks, dinner wasn't the least bit appealing. Speaking from experience, containing them to three meals and two snacks, if possible, will make them appreciate meals and be more apt to try the new foods you are introducing.

Inside Your Toddler's Mind

Everything in moderation, including empowering your toddler with the freedom of self-feeding. Our toddlers always showed a bit of attachment to their snack cup, much like with a sippy cup. They began to see this as something that gave a sense of security, even as a necessity. I was trying to make life a little easier (can you blame me?), while also instilling a sense of independence and making it easier to allow them to self-feed. I didn't realize they would turn into serial snackers!

What to Do

SET A SCHEDULE. If you're finding snack cup overuse a recurring issue, implement a food schedule that works for you and your little one. We generally allow a snack between breakfast and lunch and another between lunch and dinner. This gives our kids the energy they need to maintain stable blood sugar (and behavior) between meals, but leaves them hungry enough at mealtimes to try new tastes, textures, and deconstructed meals.

REGULATING YOUR OWN EMOTIONS AND MOODS: SNACKING BY EXAMPLE

As a stay-at-home-dad, I had my share of nonstop snacking days. I'd get bored, stop, and eat. Hit a wall on a blog post, stop, and eat. Snack, snack, snack. I realized that I had a rather unhealthy relationship with food, and my kids were mimicking my nonstop snacking behavior. I knew it was time to make a change, and so I did.

CAST AWAY THE CUP. Once your child creeps toward the end of the toddler era, you'll want to retire the snack cup. It's really only meant for them to experience the freedom of self-feeding and enhance their fine motor skills. They're probably ready for an actual bowl.

WHEN SH*T HITS THE FAN

At some point, your toddler's relationship with their snack cup or sippy cup might turn into one of comfort. Make it fun for your child to use their new cup or bowl, showing them, "Now that you're a big kid, you get a brand-new cup!" It's been easier for Evelyn because she sees her older brothers and sister using different bottles and cups on a daily basis. We always rotate what type of cup she's offered and, as a result, she's more flexible.

When Food Takes Flight

Get prepared to have your very own high-chaired mini Jackson Pollock making a masterpiece out of *your* kitchen. Every one of our kids threw food on the ground. I'm not sure that I've ever met a little one who *hasn't*. Anyone with children knows this, so don't feel horrible when chicken nuggets turn into projectiles.

Inside Your Toddler's Mind

Why do toddlers throw food? Throwing food is about the simplest form of communication—perhaps they really don't want to eat it, it looks unfamiliar, or they're simply done. Toddlers can also be selective, especially if they weren't expecting a taste or texture. To handle that, look back at some of my other food tips and tricks (pages 40–43).

There's also the possibility that they're using it to get attention, or they're afraid that if it stays on the tray, they're going to have to eat it. Floor, meet mangos!

AGES 1–2

▶ Dad isn't listening to me? Food on floor. I want down? Food on floor. This food scares me? Food on floor. My seat is uncomfortable? Food on floor. My diaper is wet? Food on floor. With infinite reasons your child might throw food, breaking it down to the why may not always be possible.

AGES 2–3

▶ Toddlers between ages two and three can start to truly understand what you're saying to them. You have a greater chance of reasoning with your toddler and of them understanding cause and effect, and hopefully these conversations will result in more of the food ending up in their mouth instead of streaking the walls.

What to Do

BE AWARE OF AMOUNTS. One of the best ways to cut down on the amount of food being thrown is to give your toddler less food in the first place. It falls into the category of common sense: The rocket can't launch if it's out of fuel.

CHEWING, NOT CHUCKING. Try sitting down with your toddler as he's buckled into his high chair and eating with him. Toddlers are big-time mimickers, so if they see you eating—and not throwing—they're more likely to do the same.

REGULATING YOUR OWN EMOTIONS AND MOODS: HIGH CHAIR LESSONS

There were times that I took pride in *loading up* the tray on my toddler's high chair, thinking this would save me from having to load up a second tray. Take it from me, making a second trip is better than getting frustrated by having to clean up three-quarters of their lunch off the floor.

TEACHABLE PARENT TOOLS TO DEPLOY

PREP YOUR FLOOR. While we were going through this messy time, I often laid down what I used to call the "hazmat," essentially a courtesy plastic tablecloth for the floor. It can be easily wiped down, *or* you can do what I do and take it out back and hit it with the hose (in true dad style).

WHEN SH*T HITS THE FAN

If your toddler continues to mutinously throw food on the floor, gentle yet firm reminders should eventually work. Instead of scolding, remind them that, "We keep the food on the tray." If all else fails, consider upgrading your toddler to a booster seat. Perhaps your pint-sized gourmet just wants a seat closer to the table—sometimes changing things up can have a surprising impact.

SLEEPING

Sleep is a big topic when you're expecting, but why are we still talking about it? Because not all transitions go smoothly when moving your toddler from bedside to their own room and into their toddler bed.

Any change is a break from routine and will likely cause some backlash. We've experienced just about every issue with transitioning kids to their own space, so delving into them here might help you with your own reluctant-yet-sleepy tod.

Co-Sleeping with the Enemy

Co-sleeping isn't something that you'll find officially recommended by many Western practitioners, but globally it's been in existence since the beginning of humankind. In child rearing, certain things work for some parents that don't work for others, but this practice allowed us to get more sleep and feel rested for the next day.

As our family grew, we adopted a laissez-faire attitude, and after four kids, I can say that we are solidly co-sleepers. It isn't something we talked about before having kids—we just found it was important for us to have our little ones close, and that it provides unique bonding time.

There is such a negative stigma associated with co-sleeping, and it's not for everyone, but if you use common sense (like using a bedside co-sleeper for infants under six months old), it can be a rewarding experience that ensures everyone gets a good night's sleep.

Inside Your Toddler's Mind

If I could get more than a few words out of our toddler, I am sure she would tell me that she loves co-sleeping. It provides her comfort through the night and a feeling of natural security and warmth. Significant research also speaks to the fact that parents' breathing and biorhythms can help lower the chance for SIDS, or sudden infant death syndrome.

AGES 1–2

▶ When we first began allowing the kids to sleep in our bed or on one of us, we would slide them into a co-sleeper (a lofted crib that pushed right up against our bed) once they fell asleep, so they could still hear us sleeping and feel our presence. We also used a middle-of-the-bed co-sleeper, which worked well, too.

AGES 2–3

▶ Once our "babies" got too big and heavy to pick up or slide across into the co-sleeper, they planted their flag smack-dab in the middle of the bed. These bigger toddlers have the ability to move when they're uncomfortable and to push a pillow or blanket away. Prepare to lose those bed-space wars around this age!

What to Do

If you decide that co-sleeping works for you, there are a few things to keep in mind:

BABIES NEED A SAFE SPACE. Babies under six months old need their own place to sleep, whether it's a crib or bassinet in your room or a co-sleeper next to you.

BABIES NEED TO SLEEP ON THEIR BACK. For the first year, babies should always sleep on their back, not on their tummy or side.

KEEP IT FIRM. Even as they age, toddlers should have a firm mattress and should not be provided with heavy blankets, fluffy pillows, or extras.

REGULATING YOUR OWN EMOTIONS AND MOODS: THE SULTRY SIDE OF SLEEP

From a parent's perspective, one of the biggest downsides of co-sleeping is that it has the ability to stifle intimacy. I do recall times that my wife and I were intimate while co-sleeping and I believe you should unlock some sort of parenting level-up achievement award after pulling off that silent and stealthy maneuver.

TEACHABLE PARENT TOOLS TO DEPLOY

EMBRACE SLEEPY ALTERNATIVES. Co-sleeping doesn't have to equal bed-sharing. If your toddler is sick or vomiting, or comes in looking for you in the night, you can set up a crib or air mattress at the side of your bed. This will keep them close while still giving you your own space.

WHEN SH*T HITS THE FAN

If co-sleeping turns out to not be your thing, begin looking into baby camera options and ways to start your kids in their own space. The next two sleep issues cover a few things you might encounter along the yawning way.

Your Presence Is Required (Not Requested)

When we transitioned our first baby to her crib, she was only a few months old. The first night, when she woke, we let her cry softly for a couple of minutes, then went in and made sure she had her pacifier, and she fell back asleep. This was the first and last crib transition that was easy for us.

When Charlie was about six months old, we tried several nights of that modified sleep training and it just *did not work*. For hours, we would go in and soothe, then soothe from the doorway, and on and on. He was wired with an inability to sleep without his mom.

In hindsight, I wonder if he was feeling the anxiety my wife and I felt at that time. We had just tragically lost our baby niece and spent time grieving, holding our kids, and not wanting to let them too far from our arms. Right or wrong, this was the birth of co-sleeping for us.

Eighteen months later, when we finally got Charlie in his own bed, it took some effort to keep him there. Night after night, I would lay on the floor next to his crib, white noise playing on my phone, just waiting. From time to time, I'd peer into his crib to see if he was asleep—half the time we met eye to eye and it scared the crap out of me.

Once he was asleep, I had to stealth crawl out of his room, but the floor creaked in certain areas, and *any* creak would stir him. Thankfully, we eventually found success.

Inside Your Toddler's Mind

Your toddler is constantly seeking safety and security, and this is just another round trip on the anxiety express. They've mastered the idea of object permanence, but they haven't mastered it with *you* yet. Whether you need to use the bathroom without an admiring audience or just slip out to let them sleep, your toddler doesn't understand that you're going to come back—you could be in the next room or in China, but you're gone.

AGES 1–2

▶ For most toddlers, the sweet spot for separation anxiety is between eighteen and twenty-four months. Adding another baby, moving to a new place, or starting a new childcare situation can cause feelings of separation anxiety to surface. As hard as it may be right now for you *and* them, they won't always need you, nor will they always be asking for you at night, so try to embrace these clingier days.

AGES 2–3

▶ Older toddlers have a greater ability to reason, see cause and effect, and self-soothe. They can also understand when you say, "Mommy and Daddy will be back in just a little bit—play with Grandma. Love you!" in a pleasant loving tone, with a promise to return. Remember, though, that having a child who is unwilling to leave you, frustrating as it can be, represents a healthy relationship between you and your toddler and is something to be embraced.

What to Do

Routines help toddlers know what's coming next even as they're dropping off to sleep, so here are some tips for success:

KEEP IT SHORT AND SWEET. I've always tried to keep the nighttime process structured and loving. Little ones need hugs, a soft and calming backrub, or a kiss. Whatever they respond to best, feeling loved is a basic ingredient to a restful night's sleep.

BRING OUT THE BOOK. Read! There's some great intel that says kids who are read to every night will have experienced a far more advanced vocabulary by the time they start kindergarten.

PROMISE TO RETURN. After our routine, I usually turn on some white noise on their sound machine and say something like, "You close your eyes, and I'll be right back in in a few minutes to check on you." Knowing that you are coming back can help ease them into the separation.

EMBRACE THE SPACED-OUT VISIT. Success with this depends on the child. With Ava, this process didn't last more than a week or two. With Charlie, it took several months of hard work, starting with, "I'll be back in one minute," and eventually increasing the times gradually to 10 minutes, by which point he was fast asleep.

REGULATING YOUR OWN EMOTIONS AND MOODS: HANDLING ANXIETY

My wife and I both have traits of obsessive-compulsive disorder and anxiety, and I do everything I can to shed my worries before I go to bed at night. Making bedtime calm and enjoyable for *everyone* is crucial to our mental health. We find it helpful to use some natural essential oils, like lavender, in diffusers (but not for babies under six months—or pets!), though there are a ton of options that can help you all sleep better.

TEACHABLE PARENT TOOLS TO DEPLOY

I'll admit there were nights I was completely drained and wasn't in the mood *at all* to put in my due dad diligence. I did all the research on this topic because of my overall frustration level when exhaustion occurs, and here are a few things that you should *never* do:

NEVER LOCK THEM IN. Don't lock them in. Not only do I find this morally wrong, but if there was an emergency, they wouldn't be able to get out. Do not lock your upset and tired child in a room so they can "self-soothe."

NEVER THREATEN PUNISHMENT BECAUSE THEY ARE CRYING. It's not helpful for anyone and can have serious consequences.

NEVER OFFER BRIBES. Although I succumbed to it occasionally in the desperate early days, I learned my lesson: I still owe Charlie an all-expenses-paid ski trip.

NEVER COME DOWN ON YOURSELF FOR CAVING AND GETTING INTO BED WITH THEM. Just don't fall asleep and stay there unless you want to make a habit of this (and if you do, that's okay too!). The point is to get your bed back, not move the circus to another room.

WHEN SH*T HITS THE FAN

Don't lose faith in the fact that things will get better. Just keep your head on straight in the meantime, minute by minute, hour by hour. When I didn't know what to do next, I switched with Jen or simply started over. I took the toddler downstairs for a glass of water, then back up to go through the routine again, even if it meant reading several books. Eventually, they conked out!

The Traveling Toddler

Once we got our kids to sleep in the crib, everything was fine. But just a month later, our toddler was crawling out of the crib and dropping down parkour style onto the carpet. It was clear what this meant: time for a toddler "big kid" bed.

Even though we had invested in 3-in-1 crib/beds to get us through the toddler years, each of our kids had trouble understanding the concept of staying in their bed now that they had the option to roam throughout the house, eventually searching for Mom and Dad's room. So what gives, wandering tod?

Inside Your Toddler's Mind

Simply put, they are scared to detach from you and your partner, and if they continue to make the trek back to your room enough times, they'll wear you down and you'll give up. Separation anxiety is the leading cause of tods refusing to stay in their beds.

AGES 1–2

▶ Persistence is key. The trauma of aloneness after sleeping close to their parents is a difficult transition. A solid, calming bedtime routine is the most effective way get them to sleep.

AGES 2–3

▶ The transition should ease once they cross the two-year-old threshold. As is true with older kids as well, the more exercise toddlers get during the day, the quicker they'll fall asleep and *stay* asleep.

What to Do

WALK THE MIDNIGHT MILE. What I like to call the Midnight Mile amounts to a battle of wills. Your toddler will get up out of bed and come to you, and each time, you'll have to walk them back. Just do it, without getting upset or showing emotion either way. In time, the process will wear your toddler down and eventually even they'll get sick of it.

DEAL WITH THE DOOR. You may choose to invest in a baby-proof doorknob cover for their room, as well as a baby video monitor to ensure they're staying safely put.

REGULATING YOUR OWN EMOTIONS AND MOODS: LAST MAN STANDING

At times, I had completely committed to not letting the kids out of their rooms—they had to fall asleep in their own bed, which meant that I would have to stay with them. I took my phone or a book and laid on the floor or sat in the chair next to them. It was a battle of wills, but I was confident that I would come out victorious, and I usually did.

TEACHABLE PARENT TOOLS TO DEPLOY

READ THE ROOM. It's important to consider exceptions, like if your toddler doesn't feel well, is tired and inconsolable, or doesn't yet have the self-control to calm themselves down. We know they won't want us near them at night forever, so we pretty much let them come into our room if they're scared, sick, or survived a bad dream.

BE MATTRESS READY. When our kids come to our room, we pull out a crib mattress, blanket, and pillow that stay under our bed so they can sleep next to us. Some mornings, I wake up and see all four of them in our room and know that I'm so lucky to have them—until they start throwing Pop-Tarts at each other at breakfast.

GET STICKER HAPPY. Consider using a sticker chart. If they accumulate stickers by staying in their bed throughout the week, perhaps they get a special weekend treat.

WHEN SH*T HITS THE FAN

If these methods don't work right away, be patient and remember that it's all about security and safety for them. At times, I've completely given up and allowed them to watch a cartoon on a tablet to lull them—it didn't do me any favors. The tablet's blue light may inhibit melatonin release and actually keep them up longer. Do what you need to do, but in the long term it's better to reinforce positive sleep patterns. (That goes for you and *your* bedtime smartphone use, too!)

GROOMING

Good grooming habits are important to instill at an early age. A toddler will likely begin to take interest, even if it's just mimicking what Mommy and Daddy are doing. They might not be able to do much more than pull their socks off or pretend to brush their hair, but you're setting the stage for them to want to leave the house looking presentable.

Getting Dressed: The Struggle Is Real

With young toddlers, sometimes the mimicry starts early! Evelyn has zero hair, but loves to wave a hairbrush or my buzzing electric toothbrush over her head. Our daily dressing routines started to show in our toddlers' behaviors, with them extending arms and legs as shirts and pants are being put on.

Mason was the easiest self-groomer and we still joke about it today. This kid woke up every morning at 6 a.m. and came downstairs to our room *completely* dressed. New underwear, jeans, shirt, socks, shoes, teeth brushed, hair combed—the whole enchilada. He was ready to go. I had no idea what to make of it. Sure, he needed help to rebrush his teeth or redo his hair occasionally, but he has his style and *owns* it.

Inside Your Toddler's Mind

As young as they are, kids may still have specific clothing needs thanks to sensory-related issues or just plain old preferences (for our Ava, that meant nothing itchy and no denim, so welcome to Leggings-town!)

TIPS & INSIGHTS

AGES 1-2

▶ This age-group doesn't put up much of a fight. Without the dexterity and strength to put on their own clothes, they're at your mercy.

▶ Dressing young toddlers in layers makes it easier to adjust to temperature changes as the day goes on.

AGES 2-3

▶ Older toddlers often become capable of getting themselves undressed for bath or bed, as well as getting dressed in simpler outfits. They'll also begin developing strong opinions on these outfits.

What to Do

CHOOSE ACCORDINGLY. Once they're able to dress themselves, consider outfits that match their abilities. Avoid buttons or tough zippers.

BE ATTENTIVE. Being available (not preoccupied) and standing by your toddlers while they dress is a great thing, but you should remind them that you're just there in case they need you.

TAKE THE TIME. When a toddler knows that you or your partner is in a hurry or need to get something done quickly, they'll resist and do the exact opposite. Try to give yourself plenty of time.

REGULATING YOUR OWN EMOTIONS AND MOODS: GO AHEAD, WE'LL CATCH UP

Toddlers don't really know how to hurry, so rushing them will just frustrate you. Consider where you're rushing to. Can you be a few minutes late? When you choose calm, the whole family dynamic will follow suit.

TEACHABLE PARENT TOOLS TO DEPLOY

BE A CLOTHING BUDDY. Help your kids gain confidence and get dressed alongside them. I laid both of our outfits on the bed and put the pieces on, one by one, with colorful commentary!

PREP YOUR CLOTHES. To plan ahead, every Sunday we do laundry. We also pull outfits for the week for everyone, with underwear, socks, and accessories included, in small metal bins labeled "Monday" through "Friday." The days are color coordinated for the younger ones, so if we say "Mason, go get the orange bin," he knows it is Tuesday.

WHEN SH*T HITS THE FAN

Once your toddler can dress and undress themselves, it's best to give them no more than two choices. We allow the kids to help choose their outfits on Sundays for the week so there isn't a fight. If they're not feeling the clothes we chose, they can switch out the bin for a different day.

My Kid Refuses to Take a Bath

Part of the routine in our house includes a daily shower or bath. It's good hygiene, but if done before bedtime, it also calms your toddler down. We love to include a few drops of lavender essential oil or epsom salts into their bath water.

Inside Your Toddler's Mind

It can be tough to get some toddlers in the bathtub. They may be fighting for control or perhaps experiencing a bit of fear. Sensory overload also tends to be a culprit in a young toddler's fear, whether it's the unique sensation of the water on their body or the temperature, so be sure it's not too hot.

70   WE'RE PARENTING A TODDLER!

AGES 1-2

▶ At this age, toys are the tops, so grab some to make it more about creative play (with a side of hair washing!).

AGES 2-3

▶ Cut down on distractions by filling the tub ahead of time with water and a few toys, so the noisy part is already done when they come in. And never leave your toddler alone near water.

What to Do

Try to get to the bottom of their apprehension. If the answer isn't obvious, then there are few things to try:

HOP IN, THE WATER'S GREAT. It's fun to have a friend in the tub; in fact, all of our kids bathed with Mom until they were five or so.

BREAK FROM ROUTINE. Consider doing a bath before dinner, rather than after. If you frame it as a special thing, their enthusiasm will increase.

GO FOR THE UPGRADE. If baths aren't cutting it anymore, consider offering them a shower. They'll see it as something only adults do, and it may feed into their desire for independence.

TEACHABLE PARENT TOOLS TO DEPLOY

GET SMART ABOUT BATH TOYS. We have a suction-cupped mesh bag that hangs and lets the bath toys drain (ones that hold water need to be dried thoroughly to prevent mold). We also hone in on fun themed toys, like boats, waterproof books, and plastic cups.

TURN TOWELS INTO COSTUMES. Instead of plain bath towels, score some that have a caped hood and resemble characters.

WHEN SH*T HITS THE FAN

Bath time seems like parenting 101, but because shit happens anyway, I'm going to issue these cautions:

BE AWARE OF APPLIANCES. Do a scan to make sure no curling irons, hair dryers, or cords are anywhere near the tub. This includes items like your phone.

NEVER LEAVE A CHILD UNATTENDED. Drowning is silent. It can happen in a matter of seconds and in as little as a few inches of water. No phone call or distraction is important enough to turn your back, even for a moment.

It's Time to Mow Those Teeth

Brushing and maintaining baby teeth is just as important as caring for adult teeth. Early good dental habits will transcend their childhood. Learning to brush is a really important skill for your toddler.

Inside Your Toddler's Mind

Your tod's brushing tolerance may vary. Some of this could come down to a sensory issue, like teething, or they may not like the flavor of toothpaste that you're using. If you're using an electric toothbrush, consider using a regular brush.

AGES 1–2

▶ Brushing teeth at this age is important for getting toddlers comfortable with the action and routine, as well as keeping those little chompers cavity-free.

AGES 2–3

▶ Kids don't really master brushing until they're six or seven years old, so these years are about conditioning them with technique and introducing them to the dentist regularly.

What to Do

MAKE BRUSHING TEETH AN EVENT. Stand elbow to elbow looking into the mirror and brush together. Bonus points if you can pull some funny faces as you're brushing!

INVENT A GAME. Do a countdown: Do 20 circles on this side and now 20 on the other! Just four scrapes across your tongue and we're all done!

GET THEM INVESTED. Let your toddler pick out their first toothbrush, creating excitement around the process. This really works when their favorite cartoon character's involved.

Here are some don'ts to save you time, money, and effort down the line:

AVOID LIQUID DURING NAPS. Liquids with a high sugar content (this includes milk!) will stick to the teeth and can eventually cause "baby bottle decay."

WATCH SUGARY DRINKS. Jen and I generally don't give our kids juice or soda because it contributes to tooth decay, and the sugar content seems to really mess with their behavior.

WHEN SH*T HITS THE FAN

If your toddler is being very stubborn, take them to your pediatric dentist for a cleaning. Have the dentist explain why it's so important to take care of your teeth. That "doctorly" influence can often do the convincing.

POTTY-TRAINING

I can't pinpoint a specific age for when it's appropriate to potty-train your kids—it's different for everyone. The best way to assess whether they are ready is by communicating and reading their signals, which might include:

▸ Can they express when they're wet?
▸ Do they hold their diaper?
▸ Can they mimic your toilet use?
▸ Do they attempt to wipe while you're changing them?
▸ Are they drawn to a training potty or capable of sitting and staying on it?

Is It Potty Time?

I'm not an expert; however, I'm a dad who's researched potty-training, worked in the parenting space for a decade, and been through this rodeo four times.

Scientifically speaking, a toddler between twelve and eighteen months has very little bladder control, so training them early isn't so much about training them, it's about training *you*.

With our family, little hints were clutch. Evelyn cried every time she peed or pooped in her diaper, so her discomfort signaled to us that she's ready to transition. Mason attempted to use the potty on his own. They would also approach the adult potty and pull at the seat or try and mimic our actions—standing up, sitting down, and pulling on the toilet paper roll.

We've had two training potties; the first, a simple red seat "bowl" that sat lower to the ground. Our second, a Fisher-Price sing-along version, played a song every time it was used, which encouraged them to keep using the potty.

Inside Your Toddler's Mind

The tricky part about being able to determine whether your kids are ready is to acknowledge their state of mind. The idea of sitting on a potty could be overwhelming (from a sensory perspective) or exciting (from an independence standpoint)—it's all uncharted waters.

AGES 1–2

▶ Acknowledging ownership over something as crazy as the potty can go a long way. If, like our Evelyn, your tod starts to approach the training potty, you'll know she's almost ready to start training. Seeing Evelyn unroll yards of toilet paper is frustrating, but we know she's growing used to the bathroom's many moving pieces!

AGES 2–3

▶ At this more developed stage, disposable training pants like Pull-Ups help bridge the gap between being ready to potty-train but not having the control to hold it while sleeping.

What to Do

GO FOR THE STAND-ALONE. A stand-alone potty with or without a dump-able (no pun intended) insert is a must. We also purchased a smaller toilet seat insert that clips onto the regular one to keep smaller tushies from falling in.

POP A SQUAT, BUTTERCUP. We began by introducing our toddlers to the idea of sitting down on the potty to pee or poop. Pee was generally what happened first, but if we got a poop, bonus!

EAT FIRST, POTTY SECOND. Our pediatrician explains that when a toddler eats or drinks, it can trigger their need to go to the bathroom. Consider using that timing to get your little one used to using the potty.

> ## REGULATING YOUR OWN EMOTIONS AND MOODS: KEEP YOUR EYE ON THE PRIZE
>
> If you can remind yourself about the light at the end of this tunnel, it might help you maintain your optimism. Once tods become potty trained, you're likely done with both buying and changing diapers—a huge milestone on many levels!

TEACHABLE PARENT TOOLS TO DEPLOY

EMBRACE THE NUDIST COLONY. This is the single best piece of advice I can give to a stay-at-home-parent breaking into the potty-training lifestyle: Keep your child pants-free when you're at home for the first few days of potty-training.

ACKNOWLEDGE THE ACCIDENTS. They'll have accidents, but the pee running down their leg will help them make the connection that *that* is what comes out, and *that* is what should be going into his potty.

TIME THE TRAINING. If you're not home 24/7, try to work on potty training on the days that you're free.

WHEN SH*T HITS THE FAN

STAY UPBEAT. Your positive demeanor will encourage them and keep things calm during the process.

PRACTICE SEMI-PRIVACY. I once set Charlie up on the adult potty with the training insert, and he asked me to "leave him alone."

Privacy and toddlers don't mix. As I returned, he met me frantically halfway, the potty-training seat stuck around his neck. To this day, I have no idea how that physically happened *or* how I got it off. It may have included some strategically deployed cooking spray, but I would never openly admit it.

The Tricky Transition to Training Pants

During the transition between diapers and underpants, you'll need to remind kids often or take them to the potty frequently. In this phase, many toddlers will require Pull-Ups.

Inside Your Toddler's Mind

Toddlers rarely make this transition without a few slips, which can be embarrassing. Do not punish them! Keeping that positive vibe going will push you over the hump!

TIPS & INSIGHTS

AGES 1-2

▶ Don't focus on milestones; instead, work with your kiddo at the speed that's right for their unique development. Training pants can be helpful in the eighteen- to twenty-four-month age range because taking diapers on and off can be cumbersome.

AGES 2-3

▶ Toddlers at this age should be growing confidence in using the potty, so keep training pants for situations like daycare, and focus the rest of your energy on building those potty skills.

What to Do

ESTABLISH A ROUTINE. As soon as they wake up, before and after they eat, before and after nap, and before bedtime are good bathroom starter times.

SET AN ALARM. I used to set my phone alarm to go off hourly to remind me to shuttle them into the bathroom. This prevented accidents and began to get them comfortable with their own potty routine.

BE WARY OF REWARD MANIPULATION. With one kid, every time they peed, we gave them a chocolate candy. They quickly learned that they could pee a bit, get candy, pee more, get more candy, and repeat. It was a lesson, and if you can do it without, I recommend that.

BUY A PLASTIC MATTRESS COVER. This will save your mattress, so just trust me on this one.

REGULATING YOUR OWN EMOTIONS AND MOODS: ACCEPT THE INEVITABLE

Plan accordingly and create a special laundry basket designated for "accident" clothes or sheets so they have priority over the "just dirty" clothes.

TEACHABLE PARENT TOOLS TO DEPLOY

TEACH GOOD AIM. Once boys are able to stand and pee, you'll have a different battle ahead of you—*aim*. Drop a few cereal pieces into the toilet and have them aim to "sink" them.

WIPE FRONT TO BACK. Front to back cuts down on any bacteria that could be introduced to the urinary tract.

TAKE IT ON THE ROAD. I said I would never "be the guy," but we started keeping a small expandable urinal in the car for road trips. This has been immeasurably handy, even as our boys have gotten older.

WHEN SH*T HITS THE FAN

KEEP CALM AND PUT TRAINING PANTS ON. Almost all of our kids made the transition within a few weeks, though one experienced a long stretch of training pants at night. Frustrating though it was, we stayed the course and in time, the training pants were retired.

THE DOCTOR WILL SEE YOU THEN. While girls generally transition quicker than boys, if your child gets to age seven and hasn't successfully made the switch, check with your physician.

Making It Through the Night Dry

Keeping dry during the day is one triumph, but then there's the Holy Grail of potty-training: stringing together multiple nights where they stay dry *all the way* through until morning.

Inside Your Toddler's Mind

Daytime potty-training is a sure victory, but nighttime presents a different challenge. Many toddlers are not developmentally ready to wake up when their bladder is full or to hold their urine for 10 or 12 hours.

Toddlers obviously don't understand that their systems aren't mature enough to stay dry all night, so it's up to us to not make a big deal of bed-wetting.

AGES 1–2

▶ Toddlers this age are generally too developmentally immature to make it through the entire night dry. Instead, focus on daytime progress.

AGES 2–3

▶ Bed-wetting may not just disappear with toddlers. Statistically, it's more common in boys (*The Journal of Pediatrics* conducted a study that revealed around 7 out of 10 bedwetters are male), and studies have shown almost 90 percent will stop on their own by age five or six. Aside from some kids having smaller bladders than others, some children may be such deep sleepers that they are unable to be awoken by the body's natural signaling response.

What to Do

BE THOUGHTFUL ABOUT DRINKS. Work toward eliminating drinks before laying down. Try and give yourself a cut-off time.

THE GENTLE REMINDER. Taking them, or reminding them to go at set times will begin to train kids' bodies to know when it's really time to go.

REGULATING YOUR OWN EMOTIONS AND MOODS: KEEP CALM AND CHANGE THE SHEETS

Yelling or scolding isn't going to help your kids make it through the night. Exercising patience until their bodies are developmentally ready to comply is your best bet.

TEACHABLE PARENT TOOLS TO DEPLOY

BE STEALTHY. If your toddler is accustomed to having underwear on during the day and is pushing back on wearing extra protection at night, you may have to wait until they're asleep and then sneak in to put it on.

TRY AN OVERNIGHT POTTY BREAK. Every night before I went to bed, I'd seat Ava, still half-asleep, on the toilet. I'd whisper to her to go potty, and she'd pee. I'd wipe her and put her back in bed.

WHEN SH*T HITS THE FAN

If you're finding yourself at a stagnant place, try switching up your strategies. It could be all about that middle-of-the-night break, where you set an alarm for 1 or 2 a.m., get up, and set them on the potty. Sometimes that's all that's needed to bridge the gap.

PLAYING

Calling what toddlers do "play" is a bit of false advertising because, for them, it's serious business. Play boosts their physical awareness, dexterity, and hand-eye coordination, but it's also about enhancing social interactions with others their age. They're building the foundations of current and future relationships!

Although toddlers are often confident in solo and parallel play, they probably don't have much experience playing with others, which includes one of the most important skills to learn: sharing.

They're slowly warming up to the concept of ownership—from things they consider "mine" to those that belong to others—but the most productive, happiest play starts with a healthy foundation of these road-tested strategies.

Sharing Is Caring

When it comes to sharing, younger toddlers have no concept of time, meaning that if you're taking something away from them, they'll perceive that it is now gone *for all of eternity*. The other roadblock is impulsiveness. No matter what it is, if they want it, it's *theirs*. Anything less than ownership means total screaming anarchy.

If your little one is having trouble sharing, ask yourself: Are they mature enough to comprehend the idea of sharing? The answer is likely a big *no*. But it's all part of growing up, and we'll explore some tips and tricks to help along the way.

Inside Your Toddler's Mind

Watching another child take away Mr. Bear, you'd think that the world was going to end. Giving it back, and giving in, seems to be the only solution to cool the fire of that toddler dragon, but remember that your toddler watches everything you do. Ultimately, the example you set is the long-term key to teaching them to share.

AGES 1-2

► At this age, a toddler isn't going to make much progress in the concept of sharing, so it's all about embracing and encouraging the fact that they're connecting objects with people.

► If they're holding tightly to something they think is theirs and another child is trying to take it away, it generally makes more sense to encourage them to hang on to it. This simple affirmation will make them feel like you understand. Pulling the toy away from a toddler this age will only exacerbate the situation.

AGES 2-3

► You'll likely begin to notice your toddler learning and growing more willing to share their possessions with others, and to trade in kind. But learning to share is a process, and they should be able to have things that are "theirs" as well. Ownership and permanence aren't always, well, permanent, but it's important that they are taught that they have some control over their things.

What to Do

SET ASIDE A PLACE FOR PLAY. Create space in your home that is just theirs, whether it's a room, a playroom, or a space within your own living room or kitchen that they know and are comfortable in.

SET THEM UP TO SHARE. Kids begin to grasp sharing around age three. Once they realize that their world won't crumble if they don't have another kid's wooden block gripped in their sweaty little hand 24/7, you'll want to continue modeling sharing in other ways. Show them that you enjoy sharing your possessions and they'll move quickly behind you to catch up.

REGULATING YOUR OWN EMOTIONS AND MOODS: TWEAKING THE GOLDEN RULE

You're not going to be able to do much for your own level of patience; however, we need to remember that not everything needs to be shared all the time. How would you feel if someone plucked your laptop from your hands and gave it to your buddy to play with? Understanding that sometimes we expect too much sharing from these little people is really important.

TEACHABLE PARENT TOOLS TO DEPLOY

BRING ON THE PRAISE. Children at this age respond well to praise. Giving up a toy to a friend or sibling on their own deserves high-fives or a hug!

KEEP YOUR COOL. I was probably too anxious with our earlier kids—I wanted to see them develop as quickly as possible. Unless they are seriously failing to thrive (something your pediatrician would tell you), let me assure you: They're good. Chill.

Sometimes your toddler wants a toy that belongs to someone else who doesn't want to share. Learning that they can't have other kids' toys all the time is valuable. If there's no sensible solution to a non-sharing standoff, separate the child from the situation or object and give them a chance to reset in a different surrounding.

Wrangling the Rough Stuff

At some point, you're going to find yourself on one side of this tricky issue: Biting. Either your kid is the one who's trying to rule the playground through force, or they're the one fending off the zombie toddler. We've only had one incident of biting, and our son was on the receiving end.

These events seem to happen less often when it's a calm playdate and are more prevalent once you've enrolled them in day care or preschool.

Most facilities have a policy toward this kind of behavior to protect the "victims," but it also opens up an opportunity for parents to address and confront the issue at home, whether you've got the victim or the "perp."

Inside Your Toddler's Mind

Your toddler is exploring their growing sense of self and fighting to express themselves. It's a battle between their wants and needs that's hobbled by their limited vocabulary and lack of impulse control. Considering that murky soup, it's no wonder kids in this age range are susceptible to outbursts and aggressive behavior. But it's not usually an indicator of future behavior, especially when it's managed correctly.

AGES 1–2

▶ At this age, toddlers start to understand the principles of the world around them. They're starving for structure, routine, and rules, and even though they may test these boundaries hourly, it's important to introduce them and be consistent.

AGES 2–3

▶ By now, communication skills have evolved in leaps and bounds, and if aggressive behavior persists, you're moving into proper discipline territory where you can apply logical consequences.

▶ Consequences should be cut with common sense; plainly put, the time should fit the crime. If they're in a ball pit and throwing balls at other kids, it makes sense to remove them until they've calmed down and understand that this isn't the proper type of behavior for this activity.

What to Do

STOP THE MADNESS. Obviously, if your toddler is involved in aggressive behavior, either as the giver or receiver, you want to extricate them from the situation immediately.

TRIAGE. Give first attention to the child who was hurt, not the one doing the hurting.

SORT IT OUT. Avoid giving your child too much attention for negative behaviors, but be sure to watch them closely afterward so you can pick up on subtle hints as to why they bit in the first place.

AVOID LABELS. Labeling your child as an "aggressor," "hitter," or "biter" implies a personal characteristic rather than an isolated incident or phase.

FIND A BALANCE. Catch them in positive moments and point out when you're proud of their behavior.

> ### REGULATING YOUR OWN EMOTIONS AND MOODS: IT GOES WITHOUT SAYING
>
> Nobody should *ever* bite a child back so that they can "see how it feels." I can't even believe that I have to say this, but I've seen it with my own eyes.

TEACHABLE PARENT TOOLS TO DEPLOY

GIVE YOUR TODDLER TOOLS. Your toddler understands so much more of what you say than they have the ability to communicate. Tell them our mouths are for eating, and we only bite food. Remind them that our arms are for hugging, not hitting. These explanations help define what they did wrong, and help them realize that if it happens again, the same consequence will arise. It may take three or four times for them to understand, but they'll eventually get it.

KEEP YOUR COOL. When biting, pulling hair, or pushing another child down or away happens, stay calm. After I've removed my toddler from a situation, I count to five inside my head before I talk to her to ground myself.

KNOW WHAT WILL BACKFIRE. Screaming, yelling, spanking, or telling your child that they've been bad isn't going to promote positive behavior; on the contrary, it's teaching them what you're trying to avoid.

TALK IT OVER. After a time-out or on the drive home, talk with your toddler about what happened. Emphasize that it's normal to have feelings of anger, but it's not okay to express them by hitting, biting, punching, or pushing.

INVESTIGATE. Knowing what to do in the situation is secondarily important to knowing what the circumstances were surrounding your child's need to be aggressive. Were they being pushed away from something they were playing with? Were they trying to get somewhere and someone wouldn't move? Look for patterns, for if you can predict your toddler's "triggers," you can learn to intervene when you spot trouble.

TEACH THE POWER OF APOLOGY. My wife and I try to ensure that apologies are meaningful, rather than just a line for them to repeat.

If aggressive behavior continues even after consistent discipline, try to analyze where this is coming from. For example, I've noticed that excessive screen time or watching something that isn't age-appropriate may be a culprit in fostering negative behaviors. Kids this age will also often mimic their parents, so if parents are constantly yelling or fighting and the little one is suddenly exhibiting more aggressive behavior, there may be a link.

MANAGING TRANSITIONS AND BEHAVIORS

Transitions are a natural part of life, and for toddlers, it's the first time they're getting a taste. They're a constant that can't be avoided: A trip to the children's museum is eventually going to come to an end, and a birthday party at the trampoline house will only last two hours. But what happens after that? How do you extract your toddler from these magical situations with the fewest casualties, and corral the stormy behavior that might come along for the ride?

The Terrible Toddler Tantrum

When I became a stay-at-home dad, tantrums were the number one reason I feared taking my kids outside the house. It's fun to take your kid out into a public setting, until it all goes sideways because you said no to a free cookie at the bakery counter. It took me a handful of trips running errands with Ava to begin to feel comfortable. Once I had a few runs under my belt, it encouraged me to expand my repertoire beyond the supermarket and into the zoo, the library, and beyond.

Inside Your Toddler's Mind

At this age, you're getting their full displeasure in its most bloodcurdling form. Kids between the ages of one and three are tantrum superstars, and when they're kicking, swinging arms, screaming, pulling off shoes and hats, or turning into deadweight, that's the moment when all the eyes around you are taking stock of your parenting abilities, or lack thereof.

What to Do

STAND STRONG AGAINST THE TANTRUM. Initially, I pandered to the tantrum and usually gave into it. I came to find out with our second child that my previous pandering was the worst thing I could've done. How quickly I forgot that *I was the adult.*

KNOW YOU'RE NOT ALONE. Most people around you are either currently parents or have been there, done that. Don't let the sanctimommies and daddies out there derail you.

> ## REGULATING YOUR OWN EMOTIONS AND MOODS: THE FRATERNITY OF DAD
>
> It's been hard for me to detach my own self from my toddler during a mega throwdown tantrum. I feel like people are looking at me, judging me (silently or not-so-silently). I vividly remember the first time I was experiencing this feeling, a dad looked over at me with an "I got ya" nod—I gratefully realized that I'd joined a fraternity of people who understood.

TEACHABLE PARENT TOOLS TO DEPLOY

THIS TRAIN WRECK IS NORMAL. Kicking, screaming, spitting, throwing haymakers, or holding their breath until they turn blue is all normal for toddlers, but you walking away can make them feel abandoned and make things worse.

DON'T SCOLD, DON'T LAUGH. I've made the mistake of snickering while my two-year-old is angry because I can't pull the rainbow out of the sky and hand it to her.

Sometimes, the best cure is to simply sit with your child and ride it out since your ability to be calm can help settle them.

REMOVE THEM IF YOU CAN. Up and leaving isn't always an option. But if you're in public and have the ability to remove them, do it.

DISTRACT, CALM, AND CHAT. Time-outs may seem like a rational punishment for creating a scene, but I find that a security item like a binky can instantly defuse the situation. Once their focus is transferred, talk over why they got so upset and suggest better ways to react. Point out that communicating is better than freaking out because you can understand what they want.

WHEN SH*T HITS THE FAN

With experience, I developed (and you will, too!) a savant-like tantrum sense.

Being able to anticipate what's going to upset your tod, and heading them off, is half the battle. Giving them a 10-minute warning and reminding them during the countdown provides an expectation and lead time on the change that's about to occur.

If they haven't had enough sleep, downtime, or food, your chances for abnormal behavior rise. A child's diet can drastically affect their mood, and studies have shown that foods with an abundance of artificial dyes and high-fructose corn syrup may contribute to hyperactivity.

The Toddler Marathon: Why Won't My Kid Stop Running Away?

If they're not strapped into something, they're racing off somewhere, and you've pretty much got to be living your life with your head on a swivel.

It doesn't matter where you are; kids love new places. As soon as you take them out of their stroller, they're off to the races with no concept of open gates, busy streets, or danger.

It's common sense, but your job is to be cautious FOR your child, both hyperaware and hypervigilant of their surroundings. Toddlers don't understand how careful they need to be in their environment. They simply don't have the ability yet to see things that could harm them.

Inside Your Toddler's Mind

Kids generally aren't running from you on purpose; they just don't know any better and they're itching to taste and touch and gnaw and drool on that *big* world out there.

AGES 1–2

▶ A "helicopter parent" takes an overprotective interest in the life of their child. Worry about not being a helicopter parent only once your kids are old enough to comprehend the dangers of their surroundings and developmentally capable of minding their own safety. With this age-group, you need to stick on them like glue.

AGES 2–3

▶ Specific directions are best. "*Stop!*" has to be one of the most confusing toddler commands. Stop what? My voice? My legs? Something like, "Evelyn, stop your feet!" or, "Evelyn, stop walking!" is a much clearer directive.

What to Do

There are a few ways to avoid the stomach-dropping feeling of losing your child in a crowded place or the anxiety of having to run after them:

KEEP THEM CONTAINED. If you're headed to the mall or an outdoor event, keep them in a front or back carrier or in their stroller. Focus on making them feel like a passenger, not a prisoner, so they don't get antsy. I always played "tour guide" for our kids, giving them a play-by-play commentary on what we were seeing.

FIND A SAFE PLACE. Scout an area where they can use those energetic little legs. They'll learn that running is okay once you've determined it's the right place and time.

REGULATING YOUR OWN EMOTIONS AND MOODS: LOSING A KID

Having a toddler run away from you is scary, but try and keep your cool. Assess the situation, locate dangerous exit points, and get to them quickly. Make an effort to alert people around you, including security if they're present. As early as possible, teach your kids to remember their own basic info (name, address, phone) and what to do if they get separated. Mason got lost inside a carnival once, but managed to keep his cool and approach a security guard, and they alerted us via loudspeaker. While I felt like an ass, I was also proud that he remembered what we taught him!

TEACHABLE PARENT TOOLS TO DEPLOY

SET THE GROUND RULES. We never felt like it was too early to talk about expectations. My wife and I have continued to do this with our kids, even into the tween era. Setting parameters before you go somewhere can thwart them from following a dangerous instinct.

CONSEQUENCES MATTER. Whatever the situation we're walking into, we're clear that there will be consequences if behavior can't be managed. It's a strategy that reminds our kids that they control how they act and if they choose a negative behavior, there will be a consequence.

STICK TO YOUR BOUNDARIES. If those expectations aren't met, we may have to leave early or face the dreaded time-out. No child wants to have a time-out in front of peers. They also learn that good behavior will result in more of these fun things.

WHEN SH*T HITS THE FAN

When my wife was growing up, her parents implemented the "three strikes and you're out" rule. It's a practice that we've employed with our own kids.

They have three strike opportunities, or warnings, and when they hit three, they lose something of consequence.

Managing the Morning Liftoff

Even with a daily routine like getting ready for day care, toddlers can throw a wrench into your plans. I find myself repeating instructions anywhere between three and five times on any given day. I try not to raise the decibel of my voice (although it's sometimes necessary with the noise), instead using touch (tapping their shoulder, putting my hand on their back) or getting up and actually walking to wherever they are in the house.

Inside Your Toddler's Mind

You've just woken up from an enjoyable slumber, warm in your jammies, and you see the toys that quite literally were in your dreams. You're all set for a day of playing. Suddenly, you're snatched out of your cozy bed, hoisted into clothes that are stiff and cold and less comfy, and whisked to the car, zooming away from the toys you were so excited to play with.

When you think of a simple morning routine from your toddler's viewpoint, it's easy to see how that's a recipe for a meltdown. Toddlers aren't yet conditioned with a sense of responsibility—that's for us to worry about.

AGES 1–2

▶ Alerting a toddler to the transition that's about to take place is really important. When our two-year-old wakes up, we say, "Oh no, we have a wet diaper! Let's change into a new dry diaper!" and, once it's time to get dressed, "I'm putting your dress on! Look at these sparkly shoes!" These simple motions can make daily transitions smoother by involving your tod.

AGES 2–3

▶ Toddlers this age can begin doing things like running to get things for you, choosing their snack for their preschool lunchbox, or following a checklist of morning to-dos. High-five and praise every effort—you have a little helper on your hands!

What to Do

PLAN AHEAD. I can't stress it enough. I've mentioned our five bins labeled "Monday" through "Friday," from which our kids pick out their clothes for the week. They have ownership of those items and are part of the decision-making process.

The bin system is one of the ways my wife and I plan and prep as best we can.

WEAVE PREP INTO YOUR ROUTINE. While my wife likes to prep for the week ahead on Sundays, this normally coincides with the occasional football game. To counter that conflict, I'm usually folding laundry during downs.

> ## REGULATING YOUR OWN EMOTIONS AND MOODS: SELF-CARE BENEFITS EVERYONE
>
> Mornings are really hard for me, mostly because I get hangry. Having a quick bite before anyone else is up allows me to find more compassion toward the kids—there's no need to start their day off with my poor attitude, right?

TEACHABLE PARENT TOOLS TO DEPLOY

ESTABLISH A COMMAND POST. Have one place where things go—one spot for day care/preschool folders, one for the lunchbox/water bottle, and one for the backpack. You'll know where to find these items and your toddler will learn, too.

GIVE YOURSELF TIME. Toddlers don't speak "rush," they speak "sloth." Allocate 20 minutes more than you think your exit routine will take.

Every day will not go exactly how you planned it. If a kid loses a shoe, it's not the end of the world. I used to keep a backup outfit (shoes included) in the back of our car just in case. Life's too short to dwell on the little missteps.

PART THREE

OUTSIDE THE DAILY ROUTINE

As soon as you have a routine down, your tod will throw you a curveball, and out the window it all goes. What happens when it's time to change it up? When your toddler begins behaving poorly, or when doctor appointments become a feared event? When you have to pack, travel, or shop? Let's identify some stuff that can go sideways and get ahead of it!

DANGEROUS
BEHAVIOR

Fortunately, you don't have to worry about your toddlers sneaking your beers out of the refrigerator or taking the car out for a joyride. Your parenting concerns are a little different right now. As time passes, parents tend to develop something that closely resembles clairvoyance, and you'll probably develop some yourself. You'll evolve the superhuman ability to look at a situation and immediately identify five potential dangers about it that need to be monitored or corrected. It's like a sixth sense. It's exhausting, but it can be very helpful.

My Toddler Puts Everything in Their Mouth

It's a fact: Toddlers love putting stuff in their mouths. Early on, their senses of taste and smell are how they learn and get a sense of the world around them. It's a normal impulse, and one most kids grow out of after their nervous and developmental systems align. We know tods can choke on various small items found around the house. But be careful about less-obvious choking hazards—dog food, aluminum foil, and small magnets are just a few items to look out for.

To keep things safe, store pet food in its own room and up off the floor until it's feeding time. In addition to the choking hazard, dogs can be territorial when it comes to their food. It's best not to get in their way while they're eating.

Inside Your Toddler's Mind

Everything toddlers see, touch, taste, smell, and hear is brand new to them. Think about what it must be like the first time a toddler sees corn. They want to rub it between their fingers to see if it's hard, squish it in their palms, rub their hands together, smell it, maybe lick some off their hands.

Cutting molars is another new experience they're having, and it can consume them. It's important to be able to recognize the signs and give them things like kid electric toothbrushes, frozen washcloths and yogurt tubes, or vibrating toys to help soothe them.

AGES 1–2

▶ Sensory play is an important part of your tod's development, and can be as simple as nontoxic crayons to color a piece of paper, an indoor water mat, or homemade edible modeling dough. All of our children loved Duplos at this age, and in warmer months, a sandbox or water table is a fun way to get your little one's senses firing on all cylinders.

AGES 2–3

▶ Once they edge closer to three years old, you can introduce things like kinetic sand or toys that help increase hand-eye coordination, like LEGO Juniors, Lincoln Logs, or Tinkertoys. Every child is different, so consider your toddler's capabilities before introducing any new toy.

What to Do

BE MOUTH ATTENTIVE. As they get older, you may want to watch to make sure that sucking or chewing behavior hasn't become something more serious, like an oral fixation related to a developmental issue. We've always given gentle reminders or replaced that item with something good to chew on.

KEEP IT IN PERSPECTIVE. Creating a huge issue out of otherwise normal behaviors is never a good option. All you'll do is embarrass your child. Yes, it's a pain to continually correct your toddler, but this is one of those things you just have to be patient with. This, too, shall pass.

REGULATING YOUR OWN EMOTIONS AND MOODS: GETTING DOWN LIFTS YOU UP

When my wife first introduced "sensory play" to the kids, it was the most fun for me! Getting down with your toddler to play LEGOs, squish up slime, or make balls with edible modeling dough—that's the fun stuff. It helps me even out my own mood when I'm having a tough day.

TEACHABLE PARENT TOOLS TO DEPLOY

FIND THE COMFORT ITEM. You might consider finding something to serve as a go-to object when the urge to chew or put items in their mouth hits them. Each of our kids had a comfort item that always served as a good distraction when we wanted to get the TV remote batteries out of their mouth.

KEEP IT CUSTOM. Ava carried a little satin fabric square and used a pacifier until she was about four. Mason started out sucking his thumb, then moved over to a stroller blanket he called his MeMe. Evelyn has nothing, but we're currently *trying* to get her hooked on something so she has a more pronounced ability to self-soothe.

DON'T BE DRASTIC. For the love of God, don't be the parent who throws out their favorite security item, cuts holes in their pacifiers, or makes them leave it for a "fairy" to take away. Let them keep it, even if it stays buried in a closet.

WHEN SH*T HITS THE FAN

Do yourself a favor: Don't ever buy just *one* of a favorite item. Otherwise, years later you'll be scouring the internet looking for "Baby Gap Blanket Satin Teddy Bear Ivory" to find a replacement. Once you know the item that brings them comfort, buy three more if you can.

My Kid Is Attracted to Danger

Even though our world still retains many of the same dangers it did 100 years ago, we're now so much more protective over our young ones. My wife is more hands-off than I am, and although it can come across as a laissez-faire approach, what she is doing is worthwhile—watchfully allowing your child to dip their toe into situations that might be risky can be a valuable tool in teaching them how to be safe from danger.

If you insulate your child so much that they never get a bruise or scraped knee, you're potentially robbing them of important childhood development. As much as it hurts in the moment, a scraped knee teaches them that even when we fall, we should get back up again.

The term "free-range parenting" typically refers to children in elementary and middle school, but it can apply to your toddler in some sense as well. Toddlers need to *feel* independent, but that doesn't mean you shouldn't be watching them. Show them, teach them, and then—from afar—supervise them. Step in if there is real danger. If they think you aren't watching, good!

Inside Your Toddler's Mind

Charlie used to run in the opposite direction as soon as we put him down. One Halloween night when he was fifteen months old and dressed as a monkey, he was buckled into an external-framed backpack. We sat it on the ground while we attended to the other two in the double stroller, glanced up, and he was *gone*, already walking toward the road. My wife dove off the sidewalk and grabbed him.

Toddlers will always find ways to declare their independence, especially when it involves running toward that shiny, dangerous thing or setting. The world is fun, an adventure, a place to be explored. They have no idea about the dangers. Our job is to be one step ahead of them at all times.

TIPS & INSIGHTS

AGES 1–2

▶ If possible, allow your young explorer to have an area of the house that is all theirs and toddler-proofed—this will be life-changing. Conversely, there are areas that are generally off-limits to toddlers, like laundry rooms and bathrooms, and these are the areas they will likely be most attracted to.

AGES 2–3

▶ Once kids are fully mobile, you've got to watch out for things like unsecured bins, chairs that lead to tables, and toilets. Older siblings' toys can contain small pieces that go in the mouth, and magnets, when swallowed, can create an extremely dangerous situation in the intestines that can require emergency surgery.

What to Do

The opportunities for childproofing are endless: Gates at stairwells, locks on kitchen and bathroom cabinets, covers on cords and electrical outlets, and stove knobs are all worth the investment. Here are a few others to consider:

▶ **Furniture and TVs.** Secure any high-standing furniture with wall mounting straps. Affix mirrors and flat-screen TVs high to the wall away from little hands.
▶ **Coffee tables.** Put glass tables in storage and cover sharp-edged ones with adhesive foam padding.
▶ **Microwaves.** Consider purchasing safety straps or locks to prevent access by toddlers.
▶ **Laundry rooms.** An open dryer can feel like an inviting warm space for your little one, so don't leave these doors open.
▶ **Animal and pet products.** Just like pet food, keep the litter box somewhere your toddler cannot easily access.
▶ **Plants.** Make sure that any plants within the reach of little chubby arms are not poisonous. Poinsettia, oleander, caladium, and mother-in-law's tongue (my favorite) can be deadly if ingested, so do your research before greening your home.
▶ **Household cleaners.** Keep these safely locked away.

REGULATING YOUR OWN EMOTIONS AND MOODS: DEALING WITH JUDGMENT

When you allow your child the freedom to experience life, it can be a challenge when other parents step in. Evelyn is small, about the size of a ten-month-old, so when she wiggles out of the cart buckle in the grocery cart and starts to stand up in the seat, shocked moms jump on me even as I say, "Yeah, she's a monkey—a year older than she looks, she's two." I may look like I don't have a clue, but I've got my eye on her and she's safe.

TEACHABLE PARENT TOOLS TO DEPLOY

TAKE A TODDLER TOUR. To curb your tod's interest in the off-limits stuff, consider showing them those things with strict supervision. Evelyn loves the perfume bottles in our bathroom, but she only gets to see them occasionally during bath time, and under my wife's watch.

OPT FOR ALL NATURAL. Consider making the switch to natural and nontoxic cleaners.

LET THEM HELP. Get them a small broom or a play vacuum. Or even hand them paper towels when you're cleaning a bathroom and let them in on the action.

Kids are attracted to danger. Ava used to bang her head—hard—on every concrete surface we passed. If we were at the pool, she would knock her forehead on the side of the pool purposefully. If we were out walking our dog, she would lean down and not-so-softly bonk her head on the asphalt. The result was a forehead constantly adorned with little bruises.

My wife and I were freaking out—surely there was something wrong with this kid! Our pediatrician said that as long as she wasn't doing real damage, it was likely her way of dealing with teething pain, and that she'd grow out of it. And in time, she did.

Stranger Danger

Like any partner would, my wife is very adamant that I never take my eyes off our kids in a public setting if I'm by myself. All it takes is a moment for someone to grab your child from the shopping cart. Jen is a reality television executive producer who's created true-crime shows. With that experience comes a wealth of truly sad firsthand knowledge about families whose lives were destroyed at the hands of predators.

One day, she called me crying, having just left Target. A man kept following her and Evelyn. He had nothing in his cart and just kept appearing in odd places. He could have been perfectly normal, or he could have been out to abduct someone. She walked out to the parking lot with a group of people, having lost sight of the man in the store. As they were walking to the car, the man appeared with no bags in tow. It was months before she went back to that store alone.

Our lesson from this: Baby-wearing is the safest bet.

Inside Your Toddler's Mind

Toddlers don't yet understand danger, and we need to be their biggest advocates in every situation. We must teach them about only trusting Mom and Dad (and extended family who are a constant in their lives). To a toddler, the world is an exciting place, not terrifying, and they don't really understand "stranger" in the sense that some people can have bad intentions.

AGES 1–2

▶ After moving to another state and starting at a new pediatric group, I was impressed when our pediatrician shook the boys' hands at our first appointment and started talking them through their examination. I hadn't considered the fact that these physicians were inherently strangers to us and our kids. He instantly put us at ease during the exam and said, "Okay, boys, I'm going to have to check your groin, but it's only okay because Dad is here and I'm a doctor, okay?" I was happy that he had the foresight to alert them that it's never okay for anyone else, much less a stranger, to touch them.

AGES 2–3

▶ Unless your child is in day care, there aren't many times when your little one is alone with people other than Mom and Dad. As they get older and head into a preschool class, they'll start to experience life apart from you. They'll meet people and see things that you aren't aware of, so it's never too early to make sure your child has a strong sense of what is acceptable from strangers and what is not.

What to Do

TEACH THEM WISELY. Some people have zero limits when it comes to engaging with your toddler. Many of these people wouldn't hurt a flea, but the problem is distinguishing between the good ones and the bad ones. It's easiest to teach your little one that we never accept anything from a stranger, and we don't talk to or follow strangers. This can also include older kids or teens who are strangers.

REGULATING YOUR OWN EMOTIONS AND MOODS: GETTING AHEAD OF DANGER

When I feel like one of my kids is in danger, I do whatever feels instinctually right in the moment. The best I can do is be vigilant and try to predict where situations could have negative outcomes. Also, educating myself on things I don't know by reading up and talking with peers helps me feel more confident about the decisions I make.

TEACHABLE PARENT TOOLS TO DEPLOY

TAKE THINGS ONLY FROM PARENTS. It may sound overprotective (and my apologies to Angela, our supermarket bakery cookie lady), but I don't want my little ones to take anything from strangers. When we get a free cookie, I take the cookie from Angela and hand it to Evelyn; that way, she sees it come from a stranger, but gets it via me.

WHEN SH*T HITS THE FAN

I once read an article about a woman in a Walmart parking lot who was handing $20 bills to women as a free "act of kindness." Turns out, the bills were laced with a chemical that caused them to pass out. One of my wife's friends posted about her own personal experience with this, walking into the store with her baby girl. Her hindsight was blistering—what would have happened if she had accepted the cash? I'm not looking to make you mistrustful of the world; I'm just saying that when you've got a kid in tow, keeping them safe is priority number one.

WELLNESS AND DOCTOR VISITS

Taking your baby to the pediatrician felt relatively easy, right? Now, you've got a toddler who wants to explore *everything* in the waiting room, including those bedraggled communal office toys. Touch toys. Lick. Drop on floor. Pick up. Lick again. Lick floor. Strep? Check. Flu? Check. We like to say this exposure boosts their immune system, but seriously?

As tiring as a doctor's visit can be, just remember it's likely your child isn't the sickest they will see that day, so you can be grateful for that. If you're a vaccine proponent, a conservative off-schedule vaccinator, or a former vaccinator, your child likely has some association with the doctor and needles, or "pricks" as our kids call them. But there are ways to keep everyone calm throughout it all, including yourself.

My Kid Is Afraid of Going to the Doctor

We've been fortunate with pediatricians who had great bedside manners, worked within engaging and interactive offices, and looked at our kids as whole children instead of a stats chart. But I've heard stories in which parents couldn't keep their kids calm at the prospect of going to the doctor. Understanding where their fear is coming from is half the battle; the other half requires action on your part to implement a plan that will help change their mind.

Inside Your Toddler's Mind

As kids near age two, they begin to develop fears. Up until this age, they've seen the doctor at fairly frequent intervals. As their memory develops, they begin to connect the dots between experiences and their outcomes.

TIPS & INSIGHTS

AGES 1-2

▶ Doctor's visits are probably not much of an issue yet. Your little one can be easily distracted and held in your arms. Sure, they can react to the stick of a needle, but they'll likely forget about it rather quickly.

AGES 2-3

▶ As kids get closer to this age bracket, their memory process starts to build, so a physician with a softer demeanor who takes the time to chat them up, show them different instruments, and explain how they're safe will yield better results.

What to Do

Here are tips to prepare for an upcoming appointment:

TALK ABOUT IT. Many children's books talk about visits to the doctor in a very positive manner. Creative play can also calm their anxiety—use some toys from a doctor's kit and help play-act the experience for your tentative tot. Let them work on you!

TIME IT RIGHT. Choose a day and time that you know your child will be rested and well-fed. Try to schedule well visits first thing in the morning, when the wait won't be as long.

BRING SUPPORT. Bring along things that will put your child at ease. This can be a special snack, their stuffed animal, or a favorite toy.

DON'T SUGARCOAT IT. We've made an effort to not give our kids unrealistic expectations. We don't lie to them or claim that certain things won't hurt.

GIVE PROPS. No matter how the visit goes, we tell our kids that they've done a good job. It might not hurt to promise a little surprise—even if it's a cookie for dessert after dinner.

REGULATING YOUR OWN EMOTIONS AND MOODS: LAUGHTER IS STILL THE BEST MEDICINE

If you seem anxious, your child will likely pick up on it. Laugh and joke with them and get them feeling silly.

TEACHABLE PARENT TOOLS TO DEPLOY

MAKE A GAME OUT OF IT. I love to ransack the doctor's office and create toys, like blowing up a doctor's glove into a high-five balloon, or pulling out an emesis (aka vomit) bag and turn it into an elephant trunk. A light-hearted approach makes a big difference.

WHEN SH*T HITS THE FAN

If you're dealing with a mega meltdown, ask a doctor or nurse to talk your toddler down. Kids can act differently sometimes when other grown-ups step in.

My Toddler Is Terrified of Getting Shots

Back when we were a family of four, Ava and Charlie were petrified of getting shots. We vaccinate on an alternative and slower schedule, and there are one or two vaccines that we chose never to give for personal reasons, but to each their own.

From the get-go, vaccines terrified our kids, and years later, not a ton has changed. Our oldest was diagnosed with systemic lupus at nine years old and as a result was subjected to weekly steroid infusions via IV. Her fear of needles was, and remains, so bad that she's had what's called vasovagal response to the stress of "a prick."

Vasovagal response is when a child faints from stressful triggers, which cause a rapid drop in heart rate and blood pressure. She has passed out in my wife's arms multiple times. This was terrifying for her and us. But once we knew this was how our child reacted, it was easier to manage her fears. We now know dozens of children who also suffer from the same reactions.

Inside Your Toddler's Mind

As grown-ups, we know that the idea of a shot is worse than an actual shot. But your toddler just knows something is going to hurt them, and that is terrifying and even paralyzing.

TIPS & INSIGHTS

AGES 1–2

▶ Young toddlers can be easily distracted and held in your arms, and they'll likely forget about any shots rather quickly. My wife would always nurse them through any shots, and pediatricians, male or female, are used to this.

AGES 2–3

▶ This age range is a bit trickier. Sometimes the best approach is simply to go, "Look, squirrel!" really loudly right at the exact moment. Distraction can be a great tool, especially since these nurses are FAST.

What to Do

NO SURPRISES. Consider talking about the appointment a few hours prior and letting them know what's going to happen. You don't have to embellish, as that will cause them to become hyperfocused on it and make the anticipation and visit worse, but it's better to let them know it's coming than to "surprise" them.

BRING SOME BACKUP. Sometimes, both of us have gone to the appointment. We've also brought along one of the grandparents if they were in town because it put the kids in a position of wanting to act like a big boy or girl.

REGULATING YOUR OWN EMOTIONS AND MOODS: ALL KIDS HAVE MELTDOWNS

I've always felt like my kids were a direct reflection of me. When your child is throwing a level-10 tantrum at the ped's office, it can make you personally feel like a failure. Keeping a level head is the most important thing you can do to reassure them—and yourself.

BE YOUR OWN BEST ADVOCATE. Many physicians will suggest that you stick to the recommended vaccination schedule. You have every right to advocate, ask questions, and discuss alternative options. My wife and I made very different decisions tailored to each of our children and their unique situations. Doctors "practice" medicine for a reason; it's not an exact science. You and your partner are your child's best medical advocate.

WHEN SH*T HITS THE FAN

If your child is paralyzed by shots, look into a topical numbing agent like lidocaine. Lidocaine is available over the counter and takes up to an hour to reach its full effect, so you may prefer to apply it before you leave for the doctor's office. Or, it can be applied at the doctor's office, where they can put a gauze patch over it so curious toddlers won't rub at it or ingest it. I try to look at the process of getting a shot like pulling off a bandage—get in, get it done quickly, and move on!

TRAVELING

Our first child was four months old before I found the confidence to pack her up and take her to the grocery store solo, so you can imagine the idea of packing up all of her stuff and traveling as a family together took some time to wrap my head around.

Taking yourself away from the security of your home base can be daunting. But with some smart preparation, it doesn't have to be the cross-country tantrum tour you might expect.

Packing for a Trip with Toddlers

We've taken our four all over by land, air, and sea. There's something amazing about introducing your kids to the love of adventure and the ability to see life through different cultures and places. We've experienced so many different cruises, waterparks, ski trips, theme parks, and historical sites—and, overall, had lots of fun. But nothing comes as close to a true kick in the pants as January 2013 and my father-in-law's sixtieth-birthday celebration.

We were driving down to rent a cabin, and the dynamic dimwitted duo (my wife and I) never checked the weather. We found ourselves driving through whiteout blizzard conditions. Using GPS, we were able to four-wheel-drive it off the interstate to try to find a hotel.

Meanwhile, we had two screaming kids, a Boston Terrier in need of a bathroom break, and a truckload of cold-weather-activity stuff in tow. After driving back and forth on the same one-mile stretch for an hour, my wife looked up and pointed out the deserted outline of a barely visible building, because the *entire town* was without power.

We made our way to the room using the flashlights on our phones, and we all slept together in chilly rooms with no heat, wolfing down packs of crackers. Without the benefits of modern technology, this was one of our most memorable trips together.

Inside Your Toddler's Mind

Going on any kind of excursion can create some nervous energy. They're away from home, their routine, and things that are familiar to them. They have to learn to embrace the feeling of "different" as a good thing and not a bad one, and this only comes from meaningful repetition.

AGES 1–2

▶ I would recommend giving up on the idea that anything is going to go according to plan. It just isn't. Toddlers have one timeline: their own. Aside from meeting hard obligations like flight times, stay flexible. It will make your experience so much more enjoyable.

AGES 2–3

▶ Whether you're traveling by air or highway, a prize box is a great idea for little ones. We keep little containers for each kid. Every hour or so, we hand them something: a coloring book and crayons, slime (for the mess factor, I don't recommend this, but my wife rarely listens to reason), special snacks, or even colorful window clings. It provides entertainment timed at perfect intervals to stave off road boredom.

What to Do

LOVE THE LIST. My wife's legit diagnosed OCD combined with her closeted joy of having our family look "together" takes control in these moments and gets us through the finish line. I'm great at laundry and mass folding, but she masterminds the entire operation. But that somewhat lopsided team effort wouldn't be possible without *the list*.

HAVE A WELL-EQUIPPED DIAPER BAG. Here's a quick starter list to keep in mind (assuming your chargers, snacks, toys, and toiletries are already packed up):

- ▸ Diapers and wipes (if you don't know this by now, I can't help you!)
- ▸ Changing pad or blanket
- ▸ Some 3- to 5-gallon baggies (for soiled clothing, liquids, etc.)
- ▸ At least two bottles or sippy cups (one will be dirty while the other is being used) and snack cups
- ▸ Hand sanitizer
- ▸ Children's pain reliever

CONDENSE WHEN POSSIBLE. We pack smart using small rolling suitcases—we use one each for our stuff and fit clothes for two kids into each suitcase. If you're on a car trip with a stopover, consider packing one "hotel bag" that has a change of clothes, pajamas, and toiletries to avoid massive unpacking of all bags mid-trip.

PACK AN EXTRA. If you're on a flight, be aware that your bags may not make it—always pack a change of clothes, pajamas, a swimsuit, toiletries, and valuable jewelry in your carry-on. When traveling with kids, you'll also want to add things like extra diapers, a swim diaper, and a jacket or sweatshirt.

DON'T FORGET THE TOD GEAR. A.K.A. the toddler sanity survival kit:

▸ Several small toys (without pieces) and a small stuffed animal
▸ Books or Kindle
▸ Tablet (charged and preloaded with games and movies), headphones, and charger
▸ Blanket (it can get cold on airplanes)

KEEP IT HANDY. We have a standard list saved, and every time a trip comes up, we lay the suitcases or bags out on the floor along with the lists. As we clean and fold laundry, we simply add things to the luggage and check them off as we go. A routine works here, too!

REGULATING YOUR OWN EMOTIONS AND MOODS: BE PREPARED

The more you prepare, the easier both the trip and keeping your cool will be. It's truly that simple. If you didn't prepare, you will inevitably get frustrated watching exits for a Dollar General to buy that critical forgotten item.

PICK AND PACK. We pack for our kids, but a few days before any trip, we pull their luggage out and invite them to pick a few items to bring along.

KEEP THE VETO POWER. Paring it down to things that will keep them comfortable and occupied is a win, but given that Charlie's Chucky doll made an appearance on our last flight and scared the daylights out of a seventy-year-old woman, we've established veto power.

WHEN SH*T HITS THE FAN

Without a doubt, you will leave something behind: a binky, blanket, or doll that your little one can't comprehend existing without. *Pack that shit first* every time—pack it first whenever you're getting ready to leave a hotel, restaurant, Grandma's house, or rest stop.

During a road trip when Ava was a toddler, I placed her special blanket along with several of her "lovies" on the roof of the car. I buckled Ava in, gave my wife the all-clear sign, and we left . . . all of her lovies scattered alongside a dark Interstate 85. I sped up and down that stretch of highway *nine times* from exit to exit until we recovered all but one. Blanket, safe; rest of the lovies, safe. Our sanity? Not so safe. Thank God we had bought extras of those little ones.

Road Trips with Toddlers

Our two oldest kids were born in Los Angeles, and with both of our families on the East Coast, we began to really think about how we would manage traveling without breaking the bank. After age two, the kids no longer qualified for the "infant in arms" clause with the airlines. We needed to start buying them seats, which quickly became prohibitively expensive. Enter the road trip.

For some parents, a road trip may seem like an overwhelming idea that you're not even remotely prepared to entertain. However, if you're willing to give the road trip a shot, I'm here to offer a few tips of organizational strategy that could (see how I said "could"?) get you there in one piece.

Inside Your Toddler's Mind

A road trip is all what you make it, so turn it into an "adventure" for your kids—this will set the stage for a memorable journey. In the beginning, your tod is excited, maybe with a tablet, coloring book, or new toy in hand. But the reality is that the newness for your toddler will wear off quickly. Their little bodies want and need to move around. They don't have any understanding of time, minutes, hours, or really even days.

AGES 1–2

▶ Frequent breaks are key. At this point, your toddler will likely still be sitting backward in their snap-in car seat. Take frequent breaks to stretch, nurse, and change diapers. Find rest stops or restaurants with indoor playgrounds where you can play tag, explore, and get some wiggles out.

AGES 2–3

▶ By now, your tod might have switched to the forward-facing seat position, which means if you have a DVD player in your vehicle, they might be able to take advantage of the show. Otherwise if they are rear facing you can hang a tablet from the headrest of their seat.

▶ Toys can keep them entertained. One of our favorite nonelectronic toys is the Boogie Board, a coloring tablet that can be erased and redrawn on.

What to Do

If you're prepared and organized, there's room to embrace the open road, hit the asphalt, and have some serious fun. Here are a handful of things we've learned along the way:

DO A VEHICLE ONCE-OVER. Bald tires, dry-rotted windshield wipers, or low fluids can put a serious wrinkle in your plans.

TAKE ADVANTAGE OF THE SPACE. One of the upsides to driving is that if you think you may need something, you can just toss it in the car. Some ideas include:

▸ Foldable umbrella stroller
▸ Night-light and simple baby monitor
▸ Portable high chair
▸ Pack 'n Play or play yard
▸ Toys
▸ Diaper caddy loaded with diapers, wipes, ointment, thermometer, meds, and emesis bags from our ped's office
▸ Portable urinal
▸ Pull-Ups/training pants
▸ Paper towels and antibacterial wipes

REGULATING YOUR OWN EMOTIONS AND MOODS: FIND YOUR HAPPY PLACE

I consider myself a road trip master. But that doesn't mean road trips make me happy. Comedy has always made me relax, so while my wife is snoozing and the kids are calm, I put in an ear bud to listen to a podcast while I drive.

TEACHABLE PARENT TOOLS TO DEPLOY

TALK IT UP. There are plenty of ways to pass the time beyond tablets and DVDs. The highway miles provide a chance to talk about the destination and things we're looking forward to experiencing when we get there.

GET THEM MAPPING. We keep a United States road map in the trunk, because as our kids got toward the end of the toddler era, they became more interested in trying to follow along with wherever we were going.

GET LOST. If you have a bit of extra time, consider taking an hour or two and "getting lost." I once allowed the kids to choose whether we went left or right, while attempting to guess what was around the next corner, like a real-life Choose Your Own Adventure experience. They got excited and felt like they were in control.

PLAY GAMES. You can find or make cool car bingo boards where your toddler looks at the pictures on their board and has to find the things out the window. This is especially great if they have someone to play against. You'll hear a lot of, "I saw it first!" screams from the back.

WHEN SH*T HITS THE FAN

No matter what mode of travel you choose, you're always going to have those moments of meltdown. Factor in time for this and, if possible, pull over and reset.

SHOPPING

I've hated shopping for as long as I can remember and put my mom through utter shopping hell! This makes me think that my kids' shopping behavior has been channeled from my youth, and that I might be getting just what I deserve. With these strategies, you'll hopefully find your own trips much less traumatic for you and your tod!

Grocery Store Trips with a Toddler

I'm the primary cook and our kids get a front-row seat as my own personal sous chefs, so it should have crossed my mind how many things you can teach your toddler on a grocery store trip. We're talking valuable life skills here, like, um, how not to steal.

Once, when Mason was a toddler, he walked through the entire store beside me, grinning from ear to ear, watching my every move, offering to help any time the situation arose.

When we got to the car, I realized his seat belt wouldn't fit. After a brief pat-down, I pulled an arsenal of contraband from his pants and pockets, with treasures ranging from gum to Reese's to Band-Aids and a rogue stick of pepperoni. From that point on, sitting in a cart was a *must*.

Inside Your Toddler's Mind

In hindsight, Mason's brief season of shoplifting was probably a great learning experience for both of us. Mason didn't understand that we had to pay for items—in his mind, we walked through the checkout and were done. So we went back into the store and the store manager kindly walked my toddler through the checkout process—he let him scan the items and then handed him a receipt and told him, "You have to make sure you have this every time you leave a store!"

TIPS & INSIGHTS

AGES 1-2

▶ Even at this age, you can include kids in the process. Although my wife and I use notes apps to streamline our trips, we like to hand Evelyn paper and a crayon to let her help check off items as we get them.

AGES 2-3

▶ Letting your child pick out items to eat can make them feel included both in the shopping process and in meal preparation. When Charlie was a toddler, I let him choose vegetables to help me prepare. Nothing could've surprised me more than when he chose the red and orange beets "because of the color." This worked out better than I ever could have anticipated—he wound up helping me prep and roast those beets, and he's been a fan ever since.

What to Do

BEFORE YOU LEAN, MAKE SURE IT'S CLEAN. At the grocery store, hit up the disinfecting wipes to wipe down your cart. As for the cart, go for the race car!

WORK FROM THE OUTSIDE IN. Urban parenting folklore advises working the perimeter of the store first, because that's where all your staples are. If you experience a breakdown and need to split, at least you've got the important stuff.

CONSIDER THE COOKIE. In a few select situations, it could be said that I'm into bribery, and this is one of them. I often head to the bakery first and snag a free cookie, as this tends to keep a toddler quiet and entertained for at least a few minutes.

REGULATING YOUR OWN EMOTIONS AND MOODS: MAKING SHOPPING FUN AGAIN

The best thing I can do is to make sure I'm organized about my mission. I need to keep a level head, but if I snag coconut popsicles to enjoy after dinner, I'll be a happier version of myself.

SOUND IT OUT. I like to use the items in the store to brush up on our words and spelling, mostly by asking the kids to sound out names they can't pronounce.

MAKE IT A GAME. I quiz our tods on shapes and the names of fruits and vegetables. This keeps their head in the game alongside me, and they'll stop asking when they can have another cookie.

WHEN SH*T HITS THE FAN

If you can't manage the stress, check with your store to see if you can order groceries online, and then pick them up or have them delivered. Sometimes a small fee is required, but if the budget allows, not having your molar-cutting toddler gnawing on the shopping cart handle can be well worth it.

Back to (Pre)School and Clothes Shopping

When our youngest was around three years old, my wife came up with the idea, which has since become a tradition, of having a one-on-one day with each kid to get them ready for school.

We make it a special day for each child. They get to pick some special pieces of clothing and a new backpack or a lunchbox. We break up the day with lunch and talk about what they're excited for in the upcoming year.

Letting them choose things and try them on makes them feel like they have some independence, but we're always there to guide them. At least one of their choices makes it to the cashier, even if that's not necessarily for school. Knowing they got their pick, they get excited.

Inside Your Toddler's Mind

Toddlers are starting to become very independent, and that includes a distinct style and clothing preferences. We've always tried to instill a strong emphasis on personal hygiene and a neat appearance. Part of that was selfish, because we wanted our kids' appearances to give off the impression that their parents had their shit together (even when a majority of the time we didn't!), but it was also to support their growing independence.

AGES 1–2

▶ Unless you want your child to wear sweatpants forever, start getting them used to many different types of clothing. They will always have favorites, but try flying some clothes under the radar to get your toddler used to them.

AGES 2–3

▶ As your toddlers grow, they may develop strong opinions about their clothes. You can listen and include them while teaching them how to dress themselves.

▶ There is certainly a limit to this, like if your child wants to wear their underwear outside their pants, or legitimately dirty clothing. It's our job as parents to guide them, and there's a fine line between independence and letting them make bad clothing decisions, or giving off the impression that you just don't care how they look.

What to Do

To encourage your toddler to dress themselves:

BE MINDFUL OF THEIR ABILITIES. Buttons and closures are complicated and often beyond little fingers' abilities. Slip-ons or shoes with elastic or Velcro closures are a great choice until they've mastered that "tie skill" themselves.

SHAKE UP THE SHOES. If possible, try to make sure that kids have at least two or three pairs of shoes each season.

In the winter, this might include a sneaker, a rain or snow boot, and a dressier shoe. In the spring, this could include water shoes that double as play shoes, a pair of flip-flops (likely not for school wear), and slip-on sneakers.

GO FOR NEUTRALS. Essentials in neutral colors (black, gray, navy, denim, brown, khaki, and white) go with any color or pattern.

QUALITY MATTERS. You can buy an inexpensive backpack or lunchbox, but chances are good it will only last a year, if that. We decided to invest in nice stainless-steel bento-style lunchboxes and we have yet to replace *any* of them.

CHOOSE GOOD SUPPLIES. Off-brand crayons, colored pencils, and markers can be impossible to get out of clothing and off walls.

REGULATING YOUR OWN EMOTIONS AND MOODS: FIND CALM WITHIN THE CHAOS

Despite our legitimate OCD tendencies, organization relaxes both me and my wife. If you've been to our house, you'll know we have a ton of stuff everywhere. But it's an organized chaos, and that makes us both calmer.

TALK ABOUT CLOTHES. I thought my wife was crazy the first time she started talking to our three-year-old about neutrals, but when our kids know that *any* color they choose can match neutrals, it helps them learn how to dress themselves.

PICK TOGETHER. Pick out some basic pieces together, and then let your toddler help select some brighter, fun pieces to go with them.

WHEN SH*T HITS THE FAN

As long as we aren't heading to a photo-heavy event like the Kulp Family Corn Pie Fest (don't ask), we let our kids assist in choosing their own clothes. Occasionally, one kid will insist on wearing shorts in 30-degree weather. As long as he has a long-sleeved shirt and jacket on, we let him try to prove to us he won't be cold, while sneaking along an extra pair of sweatpants for when his lips start turning blue.

How Much Is That Tortoise in the Window?

When our second child, Charlie, graduated from preschool, I told him I'd buy him a turtle. Although I knew that my wife and I would essentially be responsible for it, we felt it might help him understand empathy and the responsibility of caring for animals.

After we took his "turtle" home, I did some homework. It's funny now, but the shop employee neglected to tell me that we, in fact, were buying a Russian tortoise, which can live to be more than forty-five years old! Her name is Ella, and the daily care instructions I gave to my son are ones he may have to give to *his* son, because this damn creature may outlive most of us. But Charlie's been pretty good about understanding how important it is to take care of her as part of his daily routine, making pet ownership not just a cute idea but an everyday practicality for him.

Inside Your Toddler's Mind

Caring for pets and simply being around pets are vastly different, but both experiences are important to teach kids how to approach animals. It's our job to teach toddlers that certain dogs aren't always happy to be petted, that you need to first ask the pet's mom or dad if it's okay, and to extend your hand gently to see if they're receptive.

TIPS & INSIGHTS

AGES 1–2

▶ If you're a new parent with a little one at home, you're going to have your hands full. Consider putting new pets on hold for a bit. Get your animal fix by visiting shelters, playing with kittens and puppies, and taking your child to petting zoos.

AGES 2–3

▶ Our toddler has found success at copying what our older daughter does, so we can give her a scoop and she can add food to Katy and Purry's bowls. (I never learned my lesson and got my daughter two cats *after* we got Ella.) She loves to be complimented for helping, and you can see her grow through the praise.

▶ Toddlers *love hard*. If someone isn't watching, Evelyn will squeeze the cats too tightly. She thinks she's using "loving hands," but pets can feel differently. We learned this one weekend when, before anyone could grab her, Katy scratched Evelyn on the face a literal millimeter away from her eyeball. Evelyn (and parents), meet lesson.

What to Do

DEVELOP A BOND. If you already have a family pet, help develop a bond between them and your child. Encourage playtime and allow the child to help you care for the pet. Talk to your toddler about personal space and creating a place that is just for your pet. Sometimes, just like us, our pets want to be left alone, and toddlers should learn that.

REGULATING YOUR OWN EMOTIONS AND MOODS: PET READINESS

Our daughter Ava wanted a cat, and we finally adopted two kittens, Katy and Purry, in 2017. She does a great job caring for them, but she was seven when we got them, not a toddler. Toddlers can't take care of pets, so if you get your toddler a pet, its care will fall on *you*. If this would frustrate or annoy you, I'd suggest waiting a while.

TEACHABLE PARENT TOOLS TO DEPLOY

EVERYTHING HAS FEELINGS. It's important to instill in children a love for all living things. I have never been prouder of my kids than when we watched the new *Benji*, and I looked over and three of my four children were sobbing. They learned early on that animals love us, they have feelings, and they need us to protect them.

CARING IS KINDNESS. Little ones can learn a lot from caring for another living thing, learning to treat them as part of the family, taking them out to pee or for walks, and giving them food and water and treats.

WHEN SH*T HITS THE FAN

Losing a pet is a sad reality of pet ownership and a powerful lesson for everyone. It's said that kids should see a new puppy after birth and an older, loved dog pass away to help them understand the circle of life. Our kids were devastated when our dog Cooper died. Thankfully, we knew the end was coming and were able to prepare them. They got to love on him, kiss him, and hug him.

Conclusion:
Keep on Toddlin'

When we found out we were pregnant for the first time, back in 2009, I remember pressing through pregnancy books that read more like medical journals. I felt like I was studying for an exam, rather than looking forward to embarking on a wonderful journey of becoming a father and a parent.

I could've used a book like the first in this trilogy, *We're Pregnant! The First-Time Dad's Pregnancy Handbook*, to allow me to contribute to our pregnancy and feel more connected to my partner during those important nine months.

Once the baby is born, however, you're taking another giant leap. The first year of raising your child is a daunting task, and that's what I focused on in *We're Parents! The New Dad's Guide to Baby's First Year*.

As you've seen, this book covers one of the most active periods of parenting young children. Have a blast, write the best stories down (or shoot video), and when your kids don't need these lessons anymore, be sure to keep the fraternity alive by passing along the coveted, "Oh, you've gotta hear this story," to a desperate new parent.

Resources

For Fathers

City Dads Group (CityDadsGroup.com): This group brings dads together through meetups, podcasts, boot camps, and social media.

The Dad (TheDad.com): Here you'll find jokes, memes, parenting humor, and "kind, involved fathers who talk like real people."

The Dad 2.0 Summit (Dad2Summit.com): The summit is an annual gathering for "understanding and connecting with modern men" who "see fatherhood as a vital social good."

Dad or Alive (DadorAlive.com): My blog houses confessions of an unexpected stay-at-home dad and talks about everything from the ages and stages of development to what happens when Dad's in deep shit!

Daddy Style Diaries (DaddyStyleDiaries.com): This lifestyle blog is focused on fatherhood, travel, and cars.

Designer Daddy (DesignerDaddy.com): Here you'll find discussions of parenthood and fatherhood from the gay dad of an adopted son, as well as crafting projects and pop culture references.

Fatherly (Fatherly.com): This leading digital fatherhood brand seeks to "empower men to raise great kids and lead more fulfilling adult lives" through original content.

How to Be a Dad (HowToBeADad.com): This blog offers a humorous take on fatherhood and provides "you're not alone" support.

Life of Dad (LifeOfDad.com): From shows, podcasts, and even DadTV, Life of Dad provides advice on everything from gear to date night.

Lunchbox Dad (LunchboxDad.com): This site focuses on making lunchtime fun, offering ideas for bento box lunches, parenting articles, and product reviews.

Mr. Dad (MrDad.com): This site offers advice for every type, stage, and role of fatherhood, as well as product reviews and podcasts.

National At-Home Dad Network (AtHomeDad.org): Here you can find "advocacy, community, education, and support" for primary caregiving dads.

National Center for Fathering (Fathers.com): Here you'll find training, research, and even a Fathering Library designed to provide support, encouragement, and guidance.

National Fatherhood Initiative (Fatherhood.org): NFI is the "nation's leading nonprofit organization working to end father absence," and has partnered with the Armed Services, the Department of Justice, and community and charitable organizations.

Tales from the Poop Deck (TalesFromThePoopDeck.com): This cleverly titled blog discusses "navigating the stormy waters of fatherhood."

General Parenting

Babble (Babble.com): This site, courtesy of Disney, covers everything from pregnancy and parenthood to entertainment and lifestyle topics.

BabyCenter (BabyCenter.com): As the "world's number one digital parenting resource," BabyCenter reaches more than 100 million people each month and offers content in nine different languages.

Life of Mom (LifeOfMom.com): This blog brings together a community of mothers worldwide to "support and celebrate all moms."

Parenting (Parenting.com): From stroller shopping to toddler activities to fertility planning, Parenting offers guidance for nearly every step of the journey.

Parents (Parents.com): Here you'll find access to all the resources from *Parenting* magazine, as well its other publications: *Family Fun*, *Parents Latina*, *Ser Padres Bebé*, and *Ser Padres Espera*.

Very Well Family (VeryWellFamily.com): Offering a "realistic and friendly approach to pregnancy and parenting," this site has content from health care professionals about pregnancy and parenting.

WebMD (WebMD.com): A go-to online resource for medical information. Ensure you discuss all symptoms and medical issues with your physician.

What to Expect (WhatToExpect.com): What to Expect combines medically reviewed health content, lighthearted discussions, and helpful planning information to "support happy, healthy pregnancies and happy, healthy babies."

For Loss, Depression, Coping, and Parent Care

Healing Hearts, Baby Loss Comfort (BabyLossComfort.com/grief): A comprehensive collection of sites and resources (including films, Facebook pages, and children's books) are offered here for anyone affected by the loss of a child.

National Suicide Prevention Lifeline (1-800-273-TALK / 1-800-273-8255 or use their webchat on suicidepreventionlifeline.org/chat): Free and confidential support for anyone in distress and resources for professionals and loved ones.

Postpartum Dads (PostpartumDads.org): Resources, information, and firsthand guidance are offered through this website for families dealing with postpartum depression.

Postpartum Progress (PostpartumProgress.com): This site is "the world's most widely-read blog dedicated to maternal mental illness" and offers resources and support for parents dealing with postpartum- and pregnancy-related mental illnesses.

Postpartum Support International (Postpartum.net): PSI's mission is to increase awareness of postpartum-related emotional and mental changes among public and professional communities. Please note that their helpline doesn't handle emergencies.

Share: Pregnancy and Infant Loss Support (NationalShare.org): This national community is for anyone—parents, loved ones, caregivers, and professionals—who has experienced the tragic loss of a baby.

References

Faber, Adele and Elaine Mazlish. *How To Talk So Kids Will Listen & Listen So Kids Will Talk*. Scribner, 2012.

FDA.gov. "Children's Health." https://www.fda.gov/consumers /consumer-updates/childrens-health

Hargis, Aubrey. *Toddler Discipline for Every Age and Stage: Effective Strategies to Tame Tantrums, Overcome Challenges, and Help Your Child Grow*. Emeryville, CA: Rockridge Press, 2018.

Karp, Harvey. *The Happiest Toddler on the Block: How to Eliminate Tantrums and Raise a Patient, Respectful, and Cooperative One- to Four-Year-Old*. New York: Random House, 2008.

Laditan, Bunmi. *Toddlers are A**holes: It's Not Your Fault*. New York: Workman Publishing Group, Inc., 2015.

Parents.com. "Toddlers & Preschoolers." https://www.parents.com /toddlers-preschoolers/

Siegel, Daniel J. and Tina Payne Bryson. *No-Drama Discipline: The Whole-Brain Way to Calm the Chaos and Nurture Your Child's Developing Mind*. New York: Random House, 2014.

Warzak, William J., Shelby Evans, Margaret T. Floress, Amy C. Gross, and Sharon Stoolman. "Caffeine Consumption in Young Children." *The Journal of Pediatrics* 158, no. 3 (March 2011): 508–509. doi:10.1016/j.jpeds.2010.11.022

Index

Acknowledgments

If you had told my twenty-something self that I'd eventually be married with four children *and* find a way to write about the journey, I would've called you crazy. I've been blessed with finding an amazing partner, wife, and friend, Jen, to share this journey with and we've certainly helped one another weave our way through the ups and downs of becoming parents and raising a family.

Each and every day my four children teach me more about myself and help me become a better father.

Much love to my parents and siblings, Bruce, Joan, Eric, and Travis, as well as my parents-in-law, Bob and Elaine, and Jen's siblings and their partners, who have always welcomed me with open arms, love, and support (and made me an uncle seven times already!).

About the Author

Adrian Kulp has worked as a comedy booking agent for CBS, as a TV executive for Adam Sandler's Happy Madison Productions, and as vice president of development for Chelsea Handler's Borderline Amazing Productions.

For the past 10 years, he's been the voice behind the popular dad blog turned parenting memoir, *Dad or Alive: Confessions of an Unexpected Stay-at-Home Dad*. He's produced the reality series *Modern Dads* for A&E Networks, and is a partner at the largest online fatherhood community, Life of Dad, where he works on the creative team and with branded content. Kulp is also the senior executive producer of *The Ty Bentli Show* on NASH FM.

In 2018, he wrote the first book in this parenting trilogy, *We're Pregnant! The First-Time Dad's Pregnancy Handbook*, which has been a bestseller since its debut. In 2019, he followed this up with the second book, *We're Parents! The New Dad's Guide to Baby's First Year*.

FUN FACT: Kulp finished this book as their daughter cruised into her toddler years.

After 21 years in Pennsylvania, 14 years in Los Angeles, 5 years in Maryland, and 3 years in coastal Virginia, he now lives in Nashville, Tennessee, with his wife, Jen, and their four kids, Ava, Charlie, Mason, and Evelyn.

CPSIA information can be obtained
at www.ICGtesting.com
Printed in the USA
LVHW020445230320
650723LV00001B/1

9 781641 527958